CATTLE KINGS

of the

STAKED PLAINS

By

GEORGE A. WALLIS

American Guild Press

Dallas, Texas

Library of Congress Catalog Card No. 57-13188

First Edition

Printed in the United States of America by
Jewell Printing Co., Dallas

To

my son

Milton Alfred Wallis

my hope for the future

FOREWORD

The vast plateau of the Staked Plains, or *Llano Estacado,* as the Spaniards called it, is one of the greatest natural cattle countries in the world. It was a great cattle country in pre-historic times, when ancient Americans, believed to have been the Folsom men, hunted mammoths and a specie of wild cattle that is now extinct. Bones of the extinct bison and stone artifacts of the early inhabitants have been taken by archaeologists from 10,000-year-old campsites along Black Water Draw, near Portales, New Mexico.

When the Spanish explorer, Francisco Vasquez Coronado, crossed it in 1541, historians in his party wrote, "For days we saw only the sky and cattle." It was Coronado's men who put stakes down to be sure of finding their way back over the flat, sea-like terrain. Hence the name, *Llano Estacado,* or Staked Plains. Others have said that the name derived from the species of yucca which grows in abundance and has a stake-like appearance.

It was a great cattle country in 1885 when the XIT ranch, then the largest ranch in the world, extended from the northwest corner of Texas southward for 185 miles and ran 125,000 head of longhorns on its 3,000,000 acres.

It was still a great cattle country in 1951, when the Scotch-owned Matador Land and Cattle Co., Ltd., sold its 803,000 acres to an American syndicate for nineteen million dollars. H. H. "Paint" Campbell, founder of the ranch, had looked all over the western half of the United States for the ideal spot to run breeding cattle. The tremendous growth and success of the Matador was due to its location, with a network of creeks and springs which put every cow within two miles of living water.

Many of the great ranches have been broken up into smaller ranches or sold for farming purposes, but the Staked Plains will no doubt continue for many years as one of the major cattle regions of the United States.

Although the exact limits of the Staked Plains are not fully agreed upon, it extends, roughly speaking, from the Canadian River north of Amarillo, Texas, southward to the Concho bluffs in the vicinity of Midland and Odessa; and from the Pecos River in New Mexico eastward to the Caprock east of Lubbock, Texas, embracing an area approximately 150 miles wide by 200 miles long. The annual rainfall varies from 16 inches in the west to 24 inches in the east. This results in some small streams in the east but none on the western part of the plains. Running north and south, the state line divides it almost equally between New Mexico and Texas. (See map inside front cover.)

It is a great plateau, reaching an elevation of 4,500 feet above sea level at the San Juan Mesa west of Elida, New Mexico, and sloping gently toward the east to an elevation of 3,241 feet at Lubbock, Texas. All was, until recent drouth years, a vast undulating sea of grass, except the Palo Duro Canyon 20 miles south of Amarillo, Running Water Draw near Plainview, the Double Mountain fork of the Brazos near Lubbock, and the 800 foot rim of the great plateau known as the Caprock.

In writing this book, the author has tried to preserve the true story of the great ranches of this area. These ranches form the background for much of our Western literature. Although not a cowboy himself, the author believes that several years of newspaper work on the Amarillo Daily News, the Clovis News-Journal, Portales Tribune, Tucumcari Daily News, and other publications on or near the Staked Plains qualify him to make this contribution to Western history and biography. During these years he met and interviewed such famous characters as Charles Goodnight, the man who founded the first ranch of the Staked Plains; Bob Crosby, world's champion all-round cowboy; Elizabeth McCormick, belle of old Tascosa; Claude Jeffers, bronc peeler for the Matadors; Mrs. Sallie Chisum Roberts, niece and housekeeper for "Jingle Bob" John Chisum; Clifford B. Jones, former president of Texas Tech and manager of the Spur ranch, and others.

The author wishes to express his appreciation to Eugene Butler, editor of the Progressive Farmer, and to George Fitzpatrick, editor of New Mexico Magazine, who published a number of these stories on famous cattle ranches and who gave permission for the reproduction of some of the material in this volume. Also to Harry Campbell, son of "Paint" Campbell, who took time from his task of writing the history of Motley County to furnish valuable information. J. V. Hudson, H. E. Culwell, and B. Buie were generous in their response to inquiries.

GEORGE A. WALLIS

Niangua Farms
Preston, Missouri
July, 1957

CONTENTS

Foreword

ILLUSTRATIONS

These illustrations follow page 64

❧

INTRODUCTION

The ranch, as an American institution, had its birth in Texas. So did the word. Like many another item of cowboy custom, garb and vocabulary, it was adapted from the Spanish. The earliest "Texians" lived under the Mexican flag, but in their stubborn, free-souled hearts they never ceased to be American. Neither did their tongues. Their talk was naturally too terse for the linguistic subtleties of Spanish. What words they needed they borrowed—but pronounced to suit themselves. *Vaquero* became "buckeroo," *jaquima* became "hackamore," *chaparejos* became "chaps," and *rancho* or *rancheria* became "ranch."

Today every patch of western rurality spacious enough for a banty rooster to scratch in without throwing dirt through the fence is called a "ranch." We have apple, potato, peach, orange, strawberry, alfalfa, wheat, chicken, horse, sheep, goat, hog, frog and dude ranches, to mention but a few. It was not so in the beginning. Then a "ranch" was a cattle ranch, even though it might raise hundreds of horses for its own *remudas*.

Cattle have not been the only major product of ranching. Through the years cow range and ranch have produced a human breed that we of the West call "cowfolks". "Round them all up," said the late Will C. Barnes, "and you will find fewer cutbacks in the herd then among any class of people on earth." From the days of trail-driven herds out of south Texas, to the huge but fenced ranches of today there have been many changes. The longhorn is gone. The better bred Hereford fattens in his place. But the human breed of the ranches has not materially changed. It is still "cowfolks".

Ranching on the Staked Plains was a second phase of the cattle business in Texas. First: wild cattle in the south Texas brush, untended, all but ownerless until gathered and shoved up the trail to market; then the establishment of ranches, each owner with his own fairly well defined range, not only in Texas but in every section of the West where grass could be found. With the buffalo gone from the *Llano Estacado,* though the raiding redskin still lingered, the hardy "Texians," often backed by Scotch or English capital, put cattle in their place. With much of its area "so flat that a hunchback couldn't find a place to lay down," there has never been a greater cattle country in the world than the Staked Plains. The story of these ranches and the hardy "hired men on horseback" who owned, established, managed or rode for them, is a history hinged on heroism and whangy with the thews of cowboy courage. Nor were these pioneers men alone, as they had been on the trail drives. Ranch wives, mothers and daughters played their part as courageously as their menfolk.

In setting down the story of a dozen of the principal cow outfits of the Staked Plains, George Wallis has drawn most heavily upon the word-of-mouth accounts of old time cowfolks, both men and women, some of whom have passed on since he interviewed them, some still living today. Among them were Captain Charles Goodnight, Mrs. Sallie Roberts (niece of Jinglebob John Chisum), Mrs. Elizabeth McCormick (the belle of old Tascosa), Claude Jeffers (said to have ridden more broncs than any other man in the world), and W. H. Hyatt, who rode the Staked Plains longer than any other living human being, as well as many others.

Mr. Wallis himself has spent many years on and around the Staked Plains. Not an oldtimer of the oldtimers himself, he still has seen 30,000 head of cattle in one roundup, and the "dust of millin' critters" is no stranger to his nose.

He knows the land and the folks of whom he writes. Though he is too much of a "button" to have "been thar an' helped skin 'em" in the days of the open range, for that was a right smart while ago, you will read "Cattle Kings of the Staked Plains" with a sure certainty that at least he has "augured it out of the feller that was!"

—S. OMAR BARKER

Chapter I.

CHARLES GOODNIGHT AND THE JA RANCH

The Man Who Drove the Buffalo Out of Palo Duro Canyon

It was a dull gray and silent day in the fall of 1876 when two horsemen, winding their way across the vast, treeless expanse of the Staked Plains, suddenly and without forewarning of a change in the terrain, came upon the rim of a great canyon. Both were amazed at the suddenness with which they came upon the great chasm, in the midst of which appeared a boundless expanse of gamma, mesquite, and buffalo grass. Far beneath their feet this immense canyon of perpendicular cliffs and wind-swept buttes wound its way to the east. Along the floor of the gorge ran a little stream, almost concealed by giant cottonwoods. Farther back on each side of the little river hackberry and cedar dotted the breaks of the canyon.

"That's it, Pablo! That's the Palo Duro, winter home of the Comanches," Leigh Dyer, wagon boss of the Goodnight outfit, said. "*Yo pienso que si*," the Mexican replied.

"I'll bet Old Paint against your hatband that canyon was simply lousy with redskins after the first blizzard. Don't you know Colonel Mackenzie and his men had a hell of a time driving them out of that hole!"

"Are you sure the Indians are all gone?"

"I s'pose so. It has been two years since the big fight here, and most of the scattered bands should have been rounded up by this time and sent to Ft. Sill in Oklahoma."

"I hope so."

"Goodnight sent us to find a place to winter the cattle, and those cliffs will make mighty good windbreaks when the blizzards begin to howl across these plains," Dyer remarked. "Those dead cottonwoods will burn a lot better than wet buffalo chips when the snow begins to fly," he added.

The walls of the canyon appeared to be perpendicular, but they could see small herds of buffalo grazing in the valley and knew the animals must have found entrances. After proceeding along the dizzy rim for two or three miles, they found an old Indian trail that wound among ravines, slipped between huge boulders, cut along the face of high cliffs, and made a sudden descent into the canyon.

Seeing no fresh signs of Indians, they descended to explore. The buffalo herds that grazed the luxuriant grass in the valley thundered away through the brush as the cattlemen descended. Once they found tracks where a bear had scaled a wet bank as high as a man's head. A little farther along they flushed a flock of turkeys that went sailing down the creek through the cottonwood trees. Later they came upon an abandoned Indian camp in a grove.

After following the little stream for 30 or 40 miles through the great gorge it had cut, with its colored walls and wind-carved buttes, the two men emerged onto the high plateau of the Staked Plains; and the canyon was left behind. Hundreds of buffalo grazed the lowlands to the east, through which the sand-choked stream continued. Some of these had raced out of the canyon ahead of the cattlemen.

"Well, Pablo, here is where our outfit spends the winter, if Goodnight will agree," the wagon boss said.

They returned to the Mexican settlement on the Canadian River where Charles C. Goodnight and his wife, Mary Ann Dyer, the Tennessee girl he had married in 1870, were waiting with 1,600 head of cattle they had trailed from Colorado to avoid the rigors of approaching winter.

When Goodnight, who had been ranching on the Arkansas River in Colorado, heard Dyer's description of Palo Duro

Canyon with its sheltering cliffs and abundance of firewood, he bade farewell to *La Placita de la Atascosa,* or *Tascosa* as it was later called, and moved his outfit to the canyon that had recently belonged to the Comanche Indians.

Goodnight decided they would have to clear the canyon of the buffaloes. Leaving two herders with the cattle, the remaining force went to the Palo Duro and started down the canyon in a great buffalo drive. Whooping and yelling and firing their guns, the cowboys descended on the startled buffaloes. As they proceeded down the valley, there was an ever-increasing herd of the frightened beasts until it seemed there were at least 10,000 of the terrified animals thundering down the Palo Duro. The noise of the stampede rang through the canyon and re-echoed up the ravines. Great boulders were dislocated by the jar of a thousand hooves and went plungnig down the slopes, laying flat everything in their course.

At last the mouth of the canyon was reached, and the buffaloes raced out onto the open plains, leaving the Palo Duro to a new type of cattle, the Texas Longhorn.

A site near the Indian camp ground was selected for the ranch. There in a clump of cedars, using tepee poles of the Comanches for rafters, a dugout was built.

In 1876 Charles C. Goodnight thus founded the first ranch in the Panhandle of Texas.

Born March 2, 1836 in Macoupin County, Ill., he had come to Texas with his mother and step-father in 1845.

In 1855 Goodnight and a companion, J. W. Sheek, had placed their few belongings in an ox wagon and started for the gold fields of California. In Waco, they met Claiborne Varney, who offered to let the boys have 400 head of cattle to tend on the shares. Goodnight and Sheek were to receive one-fourth of the calves for looking after the cattle. The boys figured they would make about $100 each the first year, enough to support themselves. Of course their profits would be larger as their calves became cows and began to increase. Varney explained that the cattle business was like the proverbial snowball or compound interest: the farther it goes the faster the increase. Goodnight and Sheek accepted the proposition.

They took the cattle to the Palo Pinto country. Both boys had stick-to-it qualities, and at the end of eleven rather long years they had over 6,000 head of cattle. Sheek fell in love and married the daughter of one of the settlers. In 1866 Goodnight took his part of the cattle farther west, locating near where Throckmorton now stands. Indians descended on him there and stole all except 900 head.

About this time he heard that Oliver Loving of Palo Pinto was going to drive a herd to New Mexico to sell them to the United States Army. Goodnight went to see Loving and was invited to throw in his herd for the trip.

They went up the Middle Concho to its source, crossing over to the Pecos and starting up that stream to Fort Sumner, New Mexico. Indians wounded Loving, and he died at the fort on the Pecos. Goodnight sold the cattle and took the body of his partner back to Texas.

The trip to New Mexico proved to be a profitable one. Goodnight became associated with John S. Chisum, another trail driver. They drove cattle to Colorado and sold them in the mining towns. After several years of trail driving, Goodnight founded a ranch in about 1872 on the Arkansas River near where Pueblo, Colorado now stands. This was poor cow country, however, and in October of 1876 Goodnight returned to Texas, after hearing that Col. Nelson A. Miles and Col. R. S. Mackenzie had driven the Comanches out of the Panhandle, forcing them onto a reservation in Oklahoma. It was on this trip that he established the ranch in the Palo Duro Canyon, which was the predecessor to the JA Ranch.

In 1877 Leigh Dyer left the Goodnight outfit and founded the T-Anchor Ranch farther west on Palo Duro Canyon. This ranch is now the property of the West Texas State Teachers College at Canyon. The old log house that Dyer built is still standing. It is the oldest building in the Panhandle.

After ranching awhile in Palo Duro Canyon, Goodnight moved his headquarters to a more accessible location on the plains northeast of the canyon. In the early days he drove his cattle to shipping pens at Dodge City, Kansas. When the Fort Worth and Denver Railway built across his ranch in 1887, he began to ship to Fort Worth. The town of Goodnight, named for the pioneer cattleman, was located on the railroad a short time later.

As competition for control of the range increased, Goodnight began to buy and lease land south of the Palo Duro. An era of great expansion in the cattle business came on in the eighties, and in 1879 Goodnight sold an interest in his ranch to John A. Adair of England, who had opened a brokerage firm in New York and was looking for investment opportunities. Goodnight and Adair then started building up one of the largest ranches in Texas. They bought 170,000 acres of land in 1883 and acquired control of other tracts by leasing from the state. By 1888 Goodnight and Adair had 40,000 head of cattle and controlled 700,000 acres of land. The brand was changed to JA, the initials of the Englishman who was putting up the capital for the expansion.

Practically all the best beef breeds in the world originated in England and Scotland, and Adair was quick to see the superiority of the English cattle over the Texas longhorns, which had developed from Spanish stock. He encouraged

Goodnight to buy imported bulls for breeding up the cattle on the JA. The first good bulls were Shorthorns. This breed had been developed in the county of Durham, and surrounding region, of England. Progressive breeding programs and excellent pasture conditions there had made the Shorthorns the largest beef cattle in the world. The herds of the JA were greatly improved by the introduction of the blood of these larger and more heavily fleshed bulls.

Goodnight continued to manage the ranch until 1889. A big part of the land lay along Prairie Dog Creek and the Tulia in the country northeast of Plainview. Headquarters for the JA was about twelve miles northwest of where Silverton now stands.

Among the managers who followed Goodnight at the JA was Richard Walsh, an Englishman, who put the ranch on a good paying basis after some dry years and low prices in the cattle market. He left the JA to go to a ranch in South America. D. T. Hobart ran the ranch for a number of years, maintaining the quality of the cattle at a high level. Then came Monty W. Ritchie as an ownership manager. He was a descendant of the early English owners.

In 1889 Goodnight sold his interest in the ranch to his partner and went back to the region of Palo Duro Canyon. There he started building up a ranch under his exclusive ownership. During one of the roundups, a lonely old buffalo bull was brought in with the cattle. Hunters had almost exterminated these beasts for their hides. In order to prevent the bull from being killed, Goodnight had his men rope him and put a bell on him. When the next season rolled around, this monarch of the plains had collected a small harem from the ravines of Palo Duro Canyon. Goodnight fenced his range and ordered the buffalo preserved.

He made many sales from his small herd, and several buffalo hunts were staged. On one occasion young Comanches who had never seen a buffalo outside of a zoo were invited to come to the Panhandle and kill with bow and arrow the big game their forefathers had lived upon. There were 186 buffalo in the Goodnight herd in 1931.

The ranch at Goodnight was small in comparison with the JA, but it was all the pioneer cattleman needed in his declining years. Goodnight was a huge man in both his frame and his outlook on life, and he retained his vigor far beyond the traditional threescore and ten. Mrs. Goodnight died in 1926. Although the cattleman was now 90 years old, he married again in 1927. His second wife was Miss Corinne Goodnight of Butte, Montana, who may have been remotely related to the great rancher.

Goodnight moved to Clarendon in 1926. He died in 1929 at the age of 93 in Tucson, Arizona, where he had gone to spend the winter.

After his death, business men of Amarillo started a move to have the Goodnight range along the picturesque Palo Duro Canyon converted into a state park. This great chasm in the Staked Plains was already the chief playground of this growing city and was attracting artists and geologists. Other towns on the flat levels of the Plains gave their support, and the rugged Palo Duro Canyon became one of the great parks of the state.

Boys from the Civilian Conservation Corps were sent to the canyon to build roads, clean out the springs, and plant more trees. The Park Service and Highway Department took up the work where they left off. A paved road now takes the vacationist along the old Indian trail, by the Goodnight dugout, and through the red, yellow, and white cliffs of the Palo Duro. The Goodnight range and the winter home of the Comanches has become the summer playground for the large population that oil and agriculture has brought to the Staked Plains.

CHAPTER II.

C. C. SLAUGHTER'S LONG-S

From Bareback Cowboy to Owner of a Million Acre Ranch

When C. C. Slaughter, founder of the famous Long-S Ranch on the south part of the Staked Plains, started in the cattle business he was too poor to buy a saddle and had to ride bareback. This cowboy, who eventually became the owner of a million acres of land and the largest individual taxpayer in the Lone Star state, was born February 9, 1837, in Sabine County, Texas. His father, George Webb Slaughter, divided his time between farming, ranching, practicing medicine, and preaching as a circuit rider.

In 1857 the family moved to Palo Pinto, at that time on the frontier of West Texas, and started ranching with 600 head of Texas longhorns. Indians frequently raided the community, and more than once the Rev. Mr. Slaughter took his gun along while holding services at the little Baptist church in Palo Pinto.

Christopher Columbus Slaughter, generally known as C. C., had now reached the age of twenty and was anxious to do something for himself. He bought a load of cow and buffalo hides and freighted them to Jefferson, where steamboats gave connection with the outside world. On the return trip, he brought merchandise that he peddled out in Dallas and Palo Pinto. Profits from this and other trips were small, but it brought young Slaughter experience in salesmanship that proved valuable in future operations. Reverend Mr. Slaughter needed his son on the ranch, however, and soon employed him at a regular salary. The wages were small, and sometimes pay was slow.

When payday finally came, C. C. debated whether he should buy a saddle or buy cattle. In the end he took a few cows and heifers for his pay. A short time after young Slaughter made entry into the cattle business, Reverend Mr. Slaughter sent his sons to represent him at a round-up at which C. C. had to appear riding bareback. He routed his share of the longhorns from the brush, however, and did not have a fall when he was put to cutting herd riding slick.

In a pretty little grove not far from the stockade at Palo Pinto lived Cynthia Anne Jowell, belle of the frontier community. She had the accomplishments of a lady of her time —a beautiful voice, and ability to ride, shoot, and dance. Although her home was only a two-room log cabin, it was as neat and attractive as any in the settlement. And there Christopher Columbus Slaughter went courting. The hero had been to Jefferson, to the Rio Grande, and to an adjoining state. He was a prize not to be passed up, and Cynthia lost no time in accepting him when he proposed.

After they were married, they moved to a ranch back in the hills where C. C. could look after the cattle. This, too, was a modest home; but Cynthia was happy until one day the Indians came. Slaughter was away riding after the cattle when Cynthia saw the savages stealthily approaching through the bushes. She dropped the bucket she was carrying and fled to the house, pursued by a half dozen Comanches. She was fleet of foot and reached the cottage. Quickly barring the door, she seized a shotgun and prepared to fight. The crafty savages now changed their tactics. They crowded around the door and pretended that they wanted food. Opening the door cautiously, Mrs. Slaughter threw out what she had cooked. The bolt withdrawn, one of the Indians hurled himself against the door, expecting the woman to be an easy victim. He received a load of buckshot, and his companions sought shelter behind trees. Believing the report of the gun would bring help, the savages departed. Slaughter returned a few hours later and found a dead Comanche on his doorstep. He took his girl wife on the horse behind him and hurried her to Palo Pinto and safety.

C. C. joined the Palo Pinto rangers and soon became a captain of the State Rangers. Once while trailing Indians in the Devil's River country, the Rangers were close on the heels of the savages. Slaughter gave orders for his men to preserve perfect silence. They were proceeding cautiously when a buck deer sprang up and a young Ranger, forgetting himself, fired at it. The Comanches discovered their pursuers and escaped. In order to impress on his men that orders had to be obeyed, Slaughter had the ranger tied and gagged. This so infuriated the youth that when released he shot Slaughter with a buffalo gun. A bundle of buffalo hides that Slaughter had on his shoulder checked the bullet and probably saved his life. The bullet lodged in the Captain's body and bothered him throughout his life. Slaughter forgave the youth, and he remained with the Rangers, becoming one of Slaughter's best fighters and most trusted men.

About this time C. C. Slaughter became a slaveholder. Then came the Civil War. Slaughter entered the Confederate Army and so great was his courage and devotion to the cause of the Confederacy that he was promoted to the rank of colonel. One of his negro slaves, "Bill Moss Slaughter," insisted on remaining with the Slaughter family after he was freed. He spent his whole life with Long-S cattle. His last years were spent on the Quitaque ranch of R. L. Slaughter, Jr. of Lubbock, Texas. C. C. bought Bill at Waco when he was eleven years old.

Long after the Civil War, Colonel Slaughter was elected commander of the Confederate Veterans and presided over the reunion held in Dallas in 1902.

By 1868 the cattle of the Slaughter family had increased to 12,000 head. The next year they sold their entire herd to James Loving and Charles Rivers at $6.00 per head. Soon after this, the first of the railroads extending westward crossed the Missouri River into Kansas and gave connection with the East where beef had been high although it could scarcely be sold in Texas. The Slaughters and others began buying cattle and trailing them north to the shipping pens at Abilene, Kansas, following the trail laid out by Jesse Chisholm. Texas cattle rose in value. In 1870 G. W. Slaughter moved to Emporia, Kansas, in order to better look after the sale of the cattle. His son, C. C., moved to Dallas and did most of the buying. Another son, W. B. Slaughter, became boss on the trail.

The herd that went up the Chisholm trail in 1870 numbered 3,000. These brought $35.00 per head, a total of $105,000 and six times as much per head as the Slaughters had received when they sold the cattle on their ranch three years earlier. Two thousand head that were driven to Kansas the following year brought $33.00 per head or $66,000. The big cattle boom was now on. Texas longhorns were wanted to stock ranches in New Mexico, Colorado, Nebraska, and states farther north and the Slaughters did a profitable trail driving business for five years.

By 1875 the price of cattle had risen at the Texas ranches, and the trail drivers were compelled to operate on a narrow margin of profit. The elder Mr. Slaughter returned to Texas, and resumed operation of his ranch at Palo Pinto. He lived there until his death in 1895.

C. C. erected what was said to be the finest home in Dallas but the noble girl who had started with him in a log cabin in the hills of Palo Pinto did not live to enjoy it long. She died in 1876.

After his father's retirement to the old ranch at Palo Pinto, C. C. Slaughter was assisted in his trail driving operations by his brother, W. B. Slaughter. Land in eastern Kansas was rapidly being taken up by settlers. Farmers objected to having large herds of cattle driven across their small holdings, and the trail drivers had to seek another route to the north. Fortunately, another railroad was now being built along the old Santa Fe trail and had reached Fort Dodge in western Kansas. The three herds that C. C. drove north in 1877 went to Dodge City, which was established in 1872 and was for several years the largest cattle market in the world.

C. C. accompanied one of the herds. One evening they passed a Kansas settlement of "fool hoe men" as the farmers were called. These people who had come to convert the grassy plains of Kansas into farms were having a social at their new church, and C. C. and some of his men rode over to participate. The entertainment was being supervised by a young school teacher, Miss Carrie Averill. Slaughter's heart skipped a few beats the first time he saw the charming miss. He began to look around for someone to introduce him. There was some ill feeling toward the cattlemen because their stock often ate or tramped out both the grass and the crops of the homesteaders, and several persons declined to introduce Slaughter to the belle of their community.

But C. C. persevered and finally discovered a minister in the crowd, a benevolent looking old gentleman whom he asked to present him to the young lady. He took careful pains to explain that he was the son of a Baptist minister. The minister looked him over a moment and replied he guessed he could introduce him. He knew the girl all right. She was his daughter!

C. C. Slaughter and Carrie Averill were together the remainder of the evening, and after disposing of the cattle the trail driver went by to see her while on his way back to Texas. The Averills had come out to Kansas before the Civil War to see what they could do to prevent the country from becoming a slave state. Mr. Averill was somewhat skeptical of a man who had been a colonel in the Southern army, but C. C. and Carrie got along beautifully. They corresponded through the winter and were married when Slaughter came up the trail with a herd the next spring.

After 1877 C. C. Slaughter began to give more attention to cattle ranching than to trail driving. The brand he adopted was a long S lying down, and his outfit became known as the Long-S or Lazy S. He bought a herd of cows and heifers and headed toward the open prairie of West Texas to found a big ranch. The country around Abilene was still open range, but Slaughter knew that civilization would soon overtake him there. He went on west and founded the famous Long-S Ranch near where the town of Big Spring now stands. This was excellent ranch country. It was out of the tick belt, and there was no brush to interfere with working cattle. The climate was mild and cows could calve at any season of the year without loss.

The first ranch house was a dugout in a hillside with a bull hide for a door. Slaughter was quick to see the advantage of improving the native cattle. He bought 100 imported Shorthorn bulls, the first registered cattle in the Panhandle, and started breeding up the lean Texas longhorns. In 1882 he sold 1,000 three-year-old steers that averaged nearly 1,000 pounds each. These brought 7½ c a pound, or about $75 per head. This was the highest price ever received for three-year-old Texas steers at that time and remained the record for years.

Slaughter had seen the rapid settlement of Kansas and Oklahoma, and he knew that land in West Texas was certain to increase in value. When competition for control of the range became keen, he began to buy land. He bought over 200,000 acres from the Texas & Pacific Railway and in a single transaction paid them $220,485.82. In a few years the Long-S Ranch covered a large part of Howard, Dawson, Borden, and Martin counties. He also leased about 300,000 acres from the state. Early in the eighties C. C. Slaughter, J. N. Morrison, and W. D. Johnson formed the Running Water Land and Cattle Co. and started building another big ranch in Castro, Lamb, and Hale Counties. Headquarters for the ranch was on Running Water draw about 15 miles northwest of Plainview. Slaughter had a half interest in this ranch. In 1890 he traded his interest in the cattle on the ranch for the interest of his partners in the land and became full owner of this ranch of 143,000 acres.

In 1887 came the big blizzard that put many cattlemen out of business and came near bankrupting Slaughter. It was late in the afternoon when a dark blue streak appeared on the northern horizon and rapidly grew in size. Cattle on the grassy levels of the Long-S ceased grazing and, after a few sniffs of the air, started toward the rough country on Girouds Creek and the North Concho. A herd of horses that grazed along the base of Signal Mountain was rounded up by the leader and, with much kicking and neighing, galloped toward Big Spring Canyon. A perpendicular wall of black clouds, preceded by flying sand, seemed to be rolling along the prairie. Then the wind struck with a cold blast, and clouds and dust shut out the last rays of the setting sun.

In about an hour it began to snow. For three days and nights snow fell and the wind howled across the great open world of the Staked Plains. The storm struck the northern Panhandle first. A few cattle went into the breaks of the Canadian and Palo Duro Canyons and stayed on their range, but everything on the plains began to retreat before the gale. Drift fences went down like cobwebs before the weight of the herds. There were a few clear days, then more bad weather. When spring came, Slaughter had lost 10,000 head of cattle and the remnant of his herd was far down on the Pecos. Some had gone to the Rio Grande. The spring roundup was held far from home!

The moisture from the big snow brought excellent grass, however, and good calf crops followed for several seasons and helped make up the loss. Slaughter bought 246,000 acres in Cochran County west of Lubbock and founded the Whiteface Ranch. This was stocked with 20,000 cows and heifers from the old Long-S. Another ranch of 105,000 acres was established in Hudspeth County near El Paso. Other ranches were acquired in Sonora, Mexico, and in the Black Hills of South Dakota. By 1890, Slaughter owned 1,000,000 acres.

While the Shorthorns were a fine beef breed that reached great size, Slaughter found that a still better beef animal could be produced by crossing them with Herefords. His steers became famous for their size. His Whiteface ranch near Lubbock produced an animal that weighed 4,000 pounds at four years old and was for many years the world's largest steer. The steer was from a Shorthorn cow and a Hereford bull. The animal was sold to a showman who exhibited it all over the United States.

The $75 steers Slaughter had secured by using registered Shorthorn bulls with native cows had clearly demonstrated the value of fine-blooded bulls. He bought an irrigated tract in the artesian belt near Roswell, N. M., and used it as a place to raise fine bulls for his ranches. The Hereford herd at Roswell was headed by Ancient Britton, No. 55,749, a bull that took first prize at the World's Fair at Chicago in 1893. Another fine Hereford was Sir Bredwell, No. 63,685, that took first prize at the Omaha, Nebraska, Exposition in 1898. There were 24 Hereford cows on the ranch that had taken blue ribbons. The success of this ranch was largely due to the efforts of George M. Slaughter, son of the famous cattleman.

When land in West Texas increased in value, the Running Water ranch near Plainview was placed on the market for agricultural purposes. This 143,000 acre tract was soon settled with farmers from Iowa and adjoining Northern states. Today this division of the Long-S outfit is one of the finest wheat regions of the nation.

In 1909 Slaughter sold 170,000 acres of the deeded land of the old Long-S ranch north of Big Spring to the W. P. Soash Land Co., of Waterloo, Iowa. This tract brought $3,000,000. The land company resold it in small blocks for farming purposes. Over 300,000 acres of leased land was turned back to the state. This, too, was soon settled by men anxious to till the rich prairie soil. Most of this land is now in cotton.

When C. C. Slaughter died in 1919, the Long-S ranches had been reduced to about 500,000 acres. Further sales followed. Although the Slaughter heirs still run cattle on some ranches, most of the famous Long-S Ranch that once extended from Plainview to Big Spring is now in cultivation. Tractors have taken the place of the broncho in the day's work, and dairy herds graze the winter wheat where once roamed the Long-S steers.

Chapter III.

THE FARWELLS OF THE XIT

The Senator Who Founded a Ranch Four Times as Large as Rhode Island

The XIT ranch, four times as large as the state of Rhode Island and probably the largest cattle ranch in the world, was founded in 1885 when the state of Texas deeded the Capitol Land Syndicate 3,000,000 acres of land in northwest Texas in payment for erecting a magnificent capitol building at Austin.

Texas retained control of her public lands when she joined the United States in 1845 after gaining her independence from Mexico. In 1879 the state decided to raise funds for a new capitol building by selling some of this land. Opinions differed as to how much should be spent and several bills were introduced into the legislature. The one that was finally passed provided for the disposal of 3,050,-000 acres. Three million acres were to be traded for the finest building it would buy. The extra 50,000 acres, the equivalent of a good sized ranch, was to be sold to meet the expense of selecting and surveying the 3,000,000 acres.

The governor, the attorney general, the comptroller, and the commissioner of the land office were appointed as a committee to select the land. Out on the Staked Plains and in the northwest corner of the state was a vast region that until recently had belonged to the fierce Comanche Indians. There were a few cattle ranches in that part of the state, but very little of the land had been sold or was occupied by settlers. The land committee sent J. T. Munson to the Panhandle to select and survey 3,050,000 acres under a contract that gave him $7,440 for the job. Munson employed A. G. Wiley as chief surveyor, and the work of selecting the 3,050,000 acres from the public domain started in 1879. The surveyors were accompanied by five rangers who were to protect them from Indians and outlaws. The land was to be blocked in leagues of 4,428 acres each.

After examining the land in the northwest corner of the state, the party decided to make the Texas-New Mexico line the western boundary of the tract. Starting at what was supposed to be the northwest corner of Texas, the men surveyed an area that extended southward along the state line for 185 miles. The east line was 175 miles long, and the north line was 30 miles. The south and east lines were made very irregular so as to include only the best land, and it was approximately 575 miles around the great tract set aside for the purpose of erecting the capitol building. It was about the size of the state of Connecticut and more than twice as large as Delaware.

The entire region was a great plateau, ranging from an elevation of about 2,500 feet in the south to over 4,000 in the north. The whole plain was covered with a thick sod of buffalo, gamma, and mesquite grass. The South Canadian River ran through the northern part of the tract, and some springs on the Yellow House canyon provided a limited supuly of water in the south. There was little rainfall or snow in the fall and winter, and the grass cured on the prairie like hay. The high plateau was cool enough to be free from harassing insects but not cold enough to make shelter necessary for stock. In fact, it was a natural home for cattle. Here millions of wild cattle, buffalo, had grazed until hunters killed them for their hides.

The survey was completed, and the first 50,000 acres was placed on the market in 1880 to pay the cost of selecting and surveying the whole tract into leagues. There was no railroad nearer than 200 miles, the land was considered useful for grazing purposes only, and it brought 55½ cents an acre or a total of $27,750. Texas then asked building contractors to submit plans for a capitol building in exchange for 3,000,000 acres of fertile prairie land. Matthea Schnell of Rock Island, Illinois, got the contract when he submitted architect's plans for a magnificent structure of brick and granite that would be the seventh largest building in the world and the finest state capitol in the United States.

He put up a $250,000 bond and began to look around for financial assistance to fulfill the contract. He soon sold three fourths interest in the contract to Taylor, Babcock and Company, which was composed of Abner Taylor, A. C. Babcock, and John V. and Charles B. Farwell. All were wealthy, especially the Farwells.

Senator Charles B. Farwell was born at Painted Post, New York, in 1823; and his brother, John V. Farwell, was born at the same place two years later. The Farwell family moved to Illinois in 1838 when Chicago had only 3,000 inhabitants and took up farming in Ogle County. When the two boys were old enough to strike out for themselves, they drifted to Chicago and entered the drygoods business. Both had unusual business ability; and, with the rapid growth of this city on the Great Lakes, they became wealthy. They soon had their own purchasing agents in Belfast, Manchester, and Paris. Stephen F. Austin and others had already established colonies in Texas; and when the Texas proposition was submitted to the Chicago men, they saw an opportunity to further increase their wealth by a great colonization project. They were so enthusiastic about the proposition that they bought an interest in the contract before they had seen the land they were to receive.

Babcock was sent to the Panhandle to examine the land and make plans for its development. He went to Ft. Elliot on the Canadian and hired a wagon to take him to Tascosa, which was farther west on the same stream and near the Capitol land. This wild little town had recently become the county seat of newly organized Oldham County. It was a Mexican settlement with a few American ranchers. Babcock hired the county clerk, C. B. Vivian, to go with him to inspect the land.

This was an age of great expansion in cattle ranching; and men like John S. Chisum, Richard King, and George Webb Slaughter had already made fortunes in the business. Babcock decided it would be best to use the land for a big cattle ranch until the advance in civilization should make it valuable for colonization. Babcock went over the tract from the northwest corner of Texas to the Yellow House canyon far down on the Staked Plains and wrote a glowing description of the possibilities for the world's greatest cattle ranch. He estimated that 10 acres would support a cow and that 300,000 head of cattle could be kept on the tract. He got his figures too high, but the possibilities were truly enormous. Taylor, Babcock and Company bought the remainder of the contract.

Ground was broken for the Capitol building in February of 1882. The contractors built a private railroad to bring granite from the quaries in Burnett county. There were few masons in the United States, and stone cutters were imported from Scotland. The corner stone of the building weighed 16,000 pounds, and it took 15 yoke of oxen to move it to its place on the Capitol grounds. The state deeded over part of the land as the work progressed, and stocking of the ranch began in 1885. The company that owned the ranch was known as the Capitol Land Syndicate. The expense of erecting the Capitol became double the amount estimated. Large sums were also needed to stock the ranch. John V. Farwell went to England to raise funds. There in

1885 he organized the Capitol Freehold Land and Investment Co., Ltd., with a capitol of 3,000,000 pounds or approximately $15,000,000. Among those who put up this enormous sum were the Earl of Aberdeen, Quintin Hogg, the Marquis of Tweeddale, Lord Thurlow, Edward M. Denney, Henry Setton Karr, and Sir William Ewart. The capital was in reality a loan, and the Americans never surrendered control of the ranch. During the life of the loan, directors' meetings were held in London. The last of the debentures were paid off in 1909.

The new state house was completed in April, 1888. The Syndicate had expended $3,224,593.45. The building was surpassed in splendor only by the Capitol Building in Washington, D. C. It was a beautiful structure 566.6 feet long and 288 feet wide. At 311 feet, it was taller than the Capitol at Washington.

The State of Texas gave the Capitol Land Syndicate a deed to the remainder of the 3,000,000 acres in 1888. General offices of the company were in Chicago. John V. Farwell was the general manager. B. H. Campbell, a cattleman of Wichita, Kansas, was employed as manager of the ranch. He was known throughout the state as "Barbecue" Campbell because of his brand which was B Q. Campbell began buying cattle with which to stock the ranch. When the time came to select a brand, numerous suggestions were considered. The object was to secure a brand that rustlers could not work over into something else. Ad Blocker, who came up from the Colorado River country with a herd of cows he had sold to the Syndicate, suggested the XIT. Most of the brands suggested were discarded when the cowboys designed many changes that thieves might use in burning over the brands. They struck a snag, though, when they tried XIT. When Campbell saw how nearly impossible it was to convert this brand into something where XIT could not be detected, he decided it was the best. Years after the ranch was founded, someone discovered that XIT could be made into a five pointeed star with a cross in the center; but there are few men today who can do it, even after knowing what to try. XIT is one brand rustlers never successfully burned into something else.

Most of the cows for stocking the ranch were bought from stockmen along the Colorado and Concho rivers on terms that required their delivery at Yellow House canyon. Campbell received the cattle at a spring that had been a camp for buffalo hunters. Texas men were accustomed to roping and throwing the cattle in branding them. "Barbecue", however, built a chute, packed the cows into it so tightly they could only squirm, and branded them standing up. A straight bar about 5 inches long was pressed against the side of the bawling animal five times in making the brand. After the cattled were counted and branded, they were taken farther north and loose herded a few days to get them located. Since water was more plentiful in the north, the first herds went to Buffalo Springs and the Canadian River region.

Some cattle were bought from Colorado and Kansas ranchers, but most of the stock was Texas longhorns. Buffalo Springs, in the extreme north near where Dalhart now stands; and Yellow House Spring, near the present town of Littlefield, became headquarters of the first two divisions of the ranch.

The Syndicate bought 20,000 cows the first year and by 1886 had bought or contracted for 110,721 head of cattle. It was soon found that the ranch would not support Babcock's estimate of 300,000 head, but there were between 125,000 and 150,000 head of cattle on the ranch during the decade following 1886. Cowboys were hired from the trail, and approximately 150 men were employed in the early days of the ranch. The number was reduced a little when the ranch was fenced.

At first other ranchers had as many cattle on the XIT range as the company. There was little natural protection for the stock, and the cows drifted badly when blizzards swept across the plains. The managers decided to fence the ranch to keep off the stock of other cattlemen and to prevent their own from scattering. Even the fencing of a ranch of this size was a big undertaking. Bill Metcalf got the contract to fence the north and west side of the ranch. He cut most of the post in the Palo Duro canyon a short distance east of the XIT. The barbwire was hauled from Springer, New Mexico, the nearest railway point and more than 100 miles to the west. Metcalf built 260 miles of fence. J. M. Shannon built most of the fence on the south and east side of the ranch. He hauled his wire from Colorado City, Texas; and it cost the Capitol Land Syndicate $110.00 a mile to get this part of XIT fenced. This was real fence, however, with five wires and post every ten feet. Cross fences were built as the years went by, and by 1898 the great ranch was divided into 94 pastures. For fences alone, $181,000 had been spent. The east fence was scarcely complete before some rancher who disliked to see the range fenced up came during the night and cut the wire between every post for 7 miles.

The company was still buying cattle to stock the ranch when the Farwells began to suspect that all was not right at the ranch. They sent George Findlay, a trusted employee in their drygoods business at Chicago, to investigate. Findlay could neither shoot nor ride. Many of the men who rode the range for the XIT were known to be pretty tough, and "Barbecue" Campbell was not afraid of the Devil himself. If there was any dirty work going on at the ranch, it was almost certain that the drygoods man from Chicago would find himself in a dangerous situation. But the Chicagoan tackled the job. He went to Montague, Texas, and secured the assistance of A. L. Matlock, who had a reputation for fearless prosecution of cattle rustlers in that part of the state. The two men went to the Yellow House division and began to investigate. They found several bad characters working on the ranch and suspected that they were stealing cattle from the XIT. Some cows that the company had paid a good price for were found to be stunted animals from the tick infested region of the Gulf coast. It was a hard job to buy 100,000 head of cattle and have them all be first class animals, and the Campbell-bought low grade stock that Findlay found at the XIT may have been errors that were almost certain to develop in transactions of this magnitude. Campbell and his men became angry as hornets when they found Findlay and Matlock "nosing into things." Some of the men tried to start trouble, but Findlay and Matlock refused to become involved in any kind of argument. Findlay made his report to the Farwells and received a telegram to take charge of the ranch. Campbell left for Wichita, Kansas; and most of the cowboys quit or went on a strike. Findlay discharged those that seemed unruly and started the big task of building up a loyal organization.

The great XIT now had a drygoods merchant for a general manager. The cowboys told tales of how Findlay, watching a steer chewing his cud, declared that he knew there was something wrong with the animal because it had been chewing half an hour without taking a bite of anything.

The new general manager issued a set of new and stringent regulations. These were posted at the headquarters of each division. They made it an offense punishable by discharge for any cowboy to carry a pistol, dagger, or knucks. No employee was allowed to have any cattle on the ranch. No puncher could keep more than two horses of his own, and he was not allowed to feed company grain to these. The employees were forbidden to shoot antelope or capture the wild horses on the ranch. Visitors were allowed to spend only one day at a division without paying board and room. Two Texas Rangers were employed to run down cattle rustlers and to take care of any of the cowboys that might become too tough for the foreman to handle. The XIT ceased to be anything like a typical cow ranch. It became efficient, but it lost a lot of good will.

A. G. Boyce took charge of the ranch in 1887 and continued the reorganization begun by Findlay. Registered Durham, Hereford, and Polled Angus bulls were introduced to breed up the native longhorns. The ranch was too large for one man to supervise, so it was divided into seven divisions. They were Buffalo Springs, Spring Lake, Middle Water, Rito Blanco, Ojo Bravo, Escarbado, and Yellow House. The Buffalo Springs division in the extreme north consisted of 400,000 acrees, while the Yellow House division in the south had 275,000 acres. Other sections ranged between these in size. A division foreman was put over each of the divisions. General Headquarters were at Buffalo Springs in the early days of the ranch.

The southern part of the ranch was 2,000 feet lower in altitude and 150 miles farther south than Buffalo Springs, and the managers soon discovered that cows and calves did better in the south where climatic conditions were milder. The Yellow House division became the main breeding ranch, while the Buffalo Springs division was reserved for the big steers. Cattle raised on the high, cool plateau of the Panhandle were far superior to the long, lean animals of the Gulf coast; but the ranchers found that cattle raised on the high plains of the Panhandle would put on weight when taken north to the Dakotas or Montana. Steers would make a better growth if taken north when young, and even a grown animal would put on as much as 200 pounds in weight. The Capitol Freehold Land and Investment Company founded ranches in South Dakota and Montana. O. C. Cato was made manger of the Montana ranch. George Findlay spent most of his time trailing steers from Texas to the North.

From 25,000 to 30,000 calves were branded each year on the XIT in Texas. In addition to XIT on the right side, the year the animal was born was branded on the shoulder. The number of the division in which the animal was raised was placed on the jaw. This number enabled Boyce to judge the value of the various divisions and the efficiency of the division foremen. The age brand simplified matters when 3 or 4-year olds were wanted. The ear mark was a swallow-fork in the right ear.

The land in Montana belonged to the United States and was subject to homestead in small tracks. It could not be bought as in Texas. The grass on the government land, however, was free to all; and the Capitol Freehold Land and Investment Company controlled their range north of Miles City by getting the watering places. Fallon was the chief shipping point for the Montana ranch. The high, cold Buffalo Springs division of the XIT in Texas was reserved as a steer pasture. The young steers were sent there to get acclimated to the cold they were soon to encounter in the North. At first the steers were sent to South Dakota. Fifteen thousand head were sent to the Black Hills in 1889. The next year 10,000 were sent to a ranch north of the Yellow Stone park. In latter years the steers went to the ranch 60 miles north of Miles City, Montana. George Findlay received the cattle from A. G. Boyce in Texas and delivered them to the Montana manager, O. C. Cato.

It took three months to trail the cattle from Buffalo Springs to Miles City. The Montana trail ran through Lamar, Colorado, and Lusk, Wyoming. The steers were usually kept on the Montana ranch two years before they were sent to the Chicago market. Cowboys on the XIT in Texas were paid $25.00 per month and board. Those on the trail received $35.00 a month.

Much of the XIT in Texas was far from water. In order that all parts of the great ranch might be grazed, numerous wells were drilled. By 1900 there were 335 wells with windmills on the ranch. The Yellow House and Spring Lake divisions became the home of the cows and calves. Middle Water was a cull ranch.

Rustlers could not change the XIT with any success, but over along the New Mexico line they stole large calves and branded them as mavericks. They even drove XIT cows back into the hills of New Mexico and watched them until the calves were old enough to wean. Then they separated the calves from their mothers and proceeded to put their own brands on them. The Escarbada division next to the rough country of the Canadian in New Mexico suffered most from the thieves. Not without cause, the Capitol Land Syndicate accused some of its neighbors of being rustlers. The little cow men said the XIT outfit was overbearing and tried to run the whole country. There were a lot of hard feelings and some killings. When someone was killed or hanged, back in those early days people did not talk about it. There were always friends on both sides, and discussion generally led to more trouble. The killings are of too recent date to be suitable for discussion; and in regard to who was killed and why, the author will say, *"Quien sabe?"* Boyce finally solved the rustling problem by making the Escarbada division a steer pasture.

The Ft. Worth and Denver railway built through the XIT Ranch in 1887, and J. J. Hagerman built the Pecos Valley line from Roswell, New Mexico, to Amarillo, Texas, a few years later. Traversed by two railroads, the land was now ready for colonization. This great ranch, the largest in the world, was placed on the market in 1900 and began to break up into smaller ranches and farm lands. By 1903 approximately 1,500,000 acres had been sold. The largest sale was that of the Yellow House division of 275,000 acres. Major George W. Littlefield bought this fine ranch for $2.00 an acre.

The last XIT cow was sold in 1912. After that date the great ranch became purely a colonization project. Offices were opened at Farwell, Texas. There Judge James D. Hamlin, with a score of assistants, engaged in converting the great ranch into prosperous farms. Land offices were also opened at Dalhart and at other towns that grew up on the ranch. The census of 1900 placed the inhabitants of the ranch at 787. Among the rapidly growing towns on land formerly part of XIT Ranch today are Dalhart, Channing, Vega, Bovina, Amherst, Olton, Muleshoe, Farwell, and Littlefield.

Wheat and grain sorphums are the chief crops in the north and central part of the famous ranch, while cotton is a big crop in the south. School houses, fertile farms, and prosperous towns have sprung up where cowboys held their roundups in the days of old. Ten counties, Dallam, Hartley, Oldham, Deaf Smith, Parmer, Castro, Bailey, Cochran, Lamb, and Hockley, have taken the place of the seven divisions of the XIT.

CHAPTER IV.

ELIZABETH McCORMICK, THE BELLE OF OLD TASCOSA

The Wild Cow Town on the Canadian.

Old Tascosa, for a decade the wildest cow town in Texas, had its beginning in 1878 when an adventurous trader came into the Panhandle, built an adobe store building on the north bank of the Canadian River and stocked it with red licker, ammunition, and canned goods.

Of course, there were already a few people in the country. Buffalo hunters had come from Ft. Dodge, Kansas, in 1874 and pitched their camp in the cottonwood grove where the Atascosa creek empties its clear waters into the muddy stream of the Canadian. A year or two later a half dozen Mexican families, led by an American who had married a daughter of the Spanish *conquistadors,* followed the river down from New Mexico and founded La Placit, across the river from the buffalo camp, where they raised horses and sheep.

Phelps White, a 21 year old cowboy, came up from the Gulf coast of Texas driving 3,500 head of cattle belonging to his uncle, Major George W. Littlefield of Gonzales. Littlefield bought out one of the Mexicans who had taken possession of a fine spring 2 miles down the Canadian from the Atascosa and founded the LIT ranch. Then Lucian Scott and William B. Lea founded the Lone Star ranch near the Mexicans, south of the river. David T. Beal and "Deacon" Bates located their ranch, which used LX for a brand, about 25 miles down the river.

There was not a town within 100 miles; and the store became a postoffice, taking its name from Atascosa Creek. The Postal Department eliminated the A, and the new town became Tascosa.

John S. Chisum, cattle king of New Mexico, put Tascosa on a cow trail when he crossed the Canadian at Tascosa while driving cattle from the Pecos River of New Mexico to the end of the railroad at Ft. Dodge, Kansas. Other herds came up from south Texas on their way north, crossed the river at Tascosa and put the town on the Montana Trail.

With two cow trails and a large ranching area to draw from, business began to pick up at Tascosa. Main street soon became a long row of saloons, gambling houses, stores, and dance halls. Supplies were hauled from Dodge City, Kansas, about 200 miles away.

When cattlemen reached Tascosa after months on the dirty trail or came in after the roundup at local ranches, they just naturally had to celebrate. Cowboys with their arms around painted women climbed on the bar of Jack Ryan's or Martin Dunn's saloon and sang songs of the range, often emphasizing the high spots with shots from a .45 Colts.

There were a few permanent inhabitants who organized that part of Texas into Oldham county in 1882 and tried to keep some semblance of law and order. They elected Cape Willingham sheriff and backed him up by making Lucius Dills, the only lawyer in that part of the Panhandle, County Judge. Temple Houston, "General Sam's bad boy," was appointed District Attorney. The "gun lawyer" faced a tough job, and he knew it. When the official who swore in Houston asked if he was ready to qualify, the lawyer replied, "Just go ahead. The devil couldn't qualify for the job I have."

The first killing at Tascosa occured when a bunch of cowboys from the trail came galloping into town to slack their thirst at Jim East's saloon. Seeing a woman feeding some chickens, one of the merrymakers drew his pistol and opened fire at the fowls. The woman looked up just in time to see a .44 aimed in her direction. Thinking she was about to be shot, she fell in a faint. Then neighbors ran, screaming that the cowboys had killed the woman. A shooting affray between men would have caused no great excitement, but the least act against a woman was unpardonable. Sheriff Willingham seized a double barrel shotgun and, accompained by Charles A. Siringo, the "Lone Star Ranger," hurried after the supposed murderer. They found the cowboys drinking in the saloon and decided it would be healthier to wait until the men came out.

When the wild cowboy finally appeared, he was told to "put 'em up quick!" He went for his gun instead, and Willingham gave him a load of buckshot. Companions of the slain man started to take part in the shooting but were restrained by a pair of Colts in the hands of Siringo.

Tascosa now had all the facilities of a town down to a graveyard on a hill overlooking the cottonwood grove and the muddy waters of the Canadian. They named it Boot Hill; because most of its inhabitants died with their boots on. During the next few years Boot Hill looked as though an epidemic of smallpox was raging.

Temple Houston, finding his job as prosecuting attorney a tough one, resigned and went back to civilization, where he ran for State Senator. He was succeeded by Lucius Dills. Sheriff Willingham was followed by Jim East.

A score of bad men had been laid to rest on Boot Hill by 1886 when the boys of the Lone Star ranch and the LX pulled off their little fracas, which landed two men in the hospital and four in Boot Hill.

The cause of the shooting has never been fully determined. Some say that cattle rustling was back of it. Others think it was just rivalry between the Lone Star and the smaller but faster shooting LX outfit. There was plenty of rivalry between these competitors, all right. Others declare that it started over a pretty girl in one of the dance halls. The petit and charming miss who is supposed to have caused all the trouble was born in Baton Rouge, La., accompanying her parents to St. Louis and finally to Dodge City, Kansas. Dodge City was at this time the great cattle market of the West. It was the chief shipping point for the big ranches that were growing up in Texas, Oklahoma and New Mexico. Cattle buyers also came there to get cows and heifers for stocking new ranches in Wyoming and Montana. Cattlemen coming up the trail to Dodge brought stories of the new town where the herds crossed the Canadian in the Panhandle of Texas. Then one day the owner of a dance hall in Tascosa came to Dodge City and offered the miss from Baton Rouge more money than she had ever seen to go down to Texas and help entertain the lonely cowboys and ranchers of the Staked Plains. There was nothing for her to do except wear pretty clothes, dance, and be admired, according to the owner of the dance hall. He pointed out that this grassy plain, once the home of millions of wild cattle or buffalos, was the greatest natural cattle country in the world; that the ranchers were growing rich; and that a pretty girl like her could take her pick for a husband in a town where there were 500 or 600 men and not a dozen marriageable women.

Under these inducements, the miss from Louisiana bought a lot of pretty dresses and caught the stage for the cow town on the Canadian. On the stage that came down that week from Dodge was another person who was to become a prominent figure in the wild town of the Lone Star state.

This was Mickie McCormick, a blue eyed, handsome, good-natured Irishman. He was the life of the party as the stage wound its way across western Kansas, Oklahoma, and northwest Texas. He told thrilling stories of the silver boom at Silver City, New Mexico, and other live towns he had seen and kept every body laughing at his Irish wit. Mickie was going down to Tascosa to deal "Monte", the chief gambling game of the West. He had money to bank his own game; he was a Prince of Monaco in a western setting. It took several days to cross the plains from Kansas to Texas, and Mickie spent most of it courting the girl who was soon to become the Belle of old Tascosa.

For several months the vivacious French miss danced and played with rough cowboys and hardy ranchers, many of whom later became millionaire cattlemen, bankers, and statesmen. She made life miserable for rival dance halls. Temple Houston, "the gun lawyer," was there as was David T. Beal, later president of the New England National Bank of Kansas City. Phelps White, who became a millionaire cattleman and banker in New Mexico, and Billy the Kid, worst of the cowboy gunmen, were frequently in Tascosa. The Kid was "on vacation" after having become the most famous figure in a great cattle war in New Mexico. He was making friendly calls on gambling houses and dance halls, and no one molested him!

The girl from Dodge had not been in Tascosa long when Ed King of the Lone Star ranch became Mickie McCormick's rival. King was a dashing, quick-draw young fellow who was especially proud of his appointment as special deputy sheriff. Then Len Woodruff, a big quiet fellow who worked for the LX outfit, took a fancy to her. In fact, the whole town was more or less in love with the miss from Baton Rouge.

The Belle of Tascosa did her best to keep peace, but it couldn't be done. Mickie McCormick diplomatically kept in the background and let the other fellows do the fighting over the girl he fully intended to marry. The LX was about 25 miles down the river from Tascosa, and Woodruff did not get up to Tascosa very often. He was a good spender when he came, however. King tried to engage all the dances with Elizabeth the second time Woodruff came calling, but the proprietor of the dance hall objected. The LX cowboy had his inning.

There was lots of rivalry between the Lone Star and the LX. The Lone Star was a big outfit that worked 40 or 50 men during the busy season. The LX was not as large but it worked some men who were already famous for their fighting qualities. The situation at Tascosa was aggravated by a cowboy strike. Although the Lone Star was paying its men $30 a month, which was $5 more than the standard wage for cow hands, one of their men organized a strike that involved most of the ranches in the Panhandle. Some of the men who lost their jobs during the strike decided to start a ranch and steal from the Lone Star ranch. This plan was to put a bar across the L and the S of the Lone Star and make it a 48. Lucian Scott and William B. Lea, owners of the LS, discovered the plot and managed to get the brand recorded in their name first. They also took out papers for every brand they could think of that the LS could be converted into. Although the owners of the LX were in no way responsible for the acts of their former employees, the Lone Star came to hate the outfit down the river. The LS ranch was not far from Tascosa, and some of the Lone Star cowboys thought the Tascosa girls belonged to them. The LX men did not get up to the town so often, but they believed in whooping it up when they came. It is said that the jealous LS men planned to clean up on the LX cowboys at a dance one night but were prevented from starting a shooting affray when the girls got on the horses behind the men from down the Canadian and escorted them to the edge of town.

This was the situation when two LX cowboys, Len Woodruff and Charley Emroy, rode into Tascosa one day and started having a good time. They were making the rounds of the dance halls and saloons when they met Ed King and John Lang of the Lone Star ranch. Whether Woodruff and Emory had drunk too much or whether King and Lang were hunting trouble, no one knows; but when Woodruff and Emory stepped from Martin Dunn's saloon about midnight, all four men started shooting. When the smoke cleared sufficiently for other townsmen to see, Ed King was laying face down in the street dead; and the other Lone Star man, John Lang, was fleeing down the street with an empty gun. Woodruff of the LX was down on his knees with a bullet through his groin, and Emory was leaning against the wall of the saloon with a slug in his lungs.

Long, the only man who had escaped uninjured, rushed into the Jim East saloon where other Lone Star cowboys were playing "Farobank" and shouted that LX men had killed Ed King. Frank Valley and Fred Chilton, friends of King, drew their guns and rushed into the street, shooting at everything that looked like an LX man. Jesse Sheets, a neutral who ran into the street to see the fun, was mistaken for an enemy and killed. While this was going on, the wounded Emory crawled into a blacksmith shop and was not discovered by the Lone Star men. The crippled Woodruff took refuge in a room behind Dunn's saloon. Valley and Chilton followed him there and began to riddle the place with bullets. Seizing a 45-70, Woodruff flung open the door and limped out, his gun streaming lead. Valley was soon killed. Chilton, the other Lone Star cowboy, backed up, shooting as he retired. Woodruff proved to be the best shot, and Chilton, too, was killed.

Bob Crosby, World's Champion All-round Cowboy, ropes a
steer in the Pendleton, Oregon Round-Up in 1927.

Bob Crosby on "Nickel Grabber", one of his best roping
horses. The battered hat was a trademark on the smiling
cowboy.

This picture of a Matador chuckwagon meal time scene was made in 1913. It is of unusual interest because in the background are seen a group of six Scottish stockholders who had come to America to visit the ranch. Seated on stool in right foreground is Murdo MacKenzie, manager of the Matador Ranch. (Picture courtesy of Ed Smith, Matador cowboy.)

Knowing the other Lone Star cowboys might join in the fight, Woodruff fled in the darkness. Using the 45-70 for a crutch, he managed to reach the home of a friend about a mile from town. The next morning Sheriff Jim East located him by the trail of blood he left behind. Woodruff was placed under arrest, but he was in such a serious condition that he could not be moved. He made bond and remained at the house of his friend under the treatment of Dr. Henry F. Hoyt, Tascosa's only physician.

The next day after the fight, three Lone Star cowboys and an innocent bystander were carried out to Boot Hill. There was no lumber in Tascosa for making coffins, the houses having been made of adobe or sun-dried bricks. The four men were wrapped in blankets and buried in the clothes in which they died. This wild cow town on the Canadian, once the county seat of what is now many counties, had no church; and the losers in the fight at Tascosa were laid to rest without any of the rites of a Christian burial. The cattlemen and town citizens stood around with their hats off, while the graves were filled. Then all returned to town, glasses tinkled, poker chips rattled, and the dances were resumed.

People did not talk much about the killing. There were men at both ranches ready to take up the quarrel, and discussion was likely to land any one in Boot Hill. Fortunately, the governor of Texas now took a hand in affairs. He recalled a detachment of Texas Rangers from hunting bandits on the Mexican border and sent them to Tascosa. They had orders to remain there indefinitely. While enforcing peace between the ranches, they rounded up rustlers and desperados who had aggravated the situation in Tascosa.

Woodruff assumed all responsibility for killing the three Lone Star men, stood trial, and was acquitted on grounds of self defense. Other LS men were watching for an excuse to kill him, however, and he thought it prudent to leave Tascosa for a while.

Mickie McCormick was now without a competent rival. He was making more money than any one in Tascosa and was envied by all the cowboys. Most of the girls had their eyes on him; but he proposed to the girl who had ridden with him on the stage from Dodge City, and Elizabeth accepted.

The miss from Louisiana gave up her pretty ball-room dresses and put on a neat gingham apron. Mickie quit dealing "Monte" and entered the more respectable livery stable business. He started a photograph business, too, in which his pretty wife helped him. Mickie McCormick was a good hunter; and, in the years that followed, he conducted many distinguished hunting parties to the distant Rockies and into Mexico.

Of course, there were still some rustlers in the country. Once a bold thief rode into Tascosa, hired the best horse in Mickie's livery stable, rode him to Amarillo on the new railroad, and sold him to the sheriff of Potter County. Imagine the chagrin of the sheriff when he found he had bought a stolen horse and had transacted business with a thief. After his arrest, the outlaw further demonstrated his skill by escaping. McCormick got his horse back when he found where the animal was, and the sheriff was left holding the sack.

One of the "Monte" decks of the famous gambler has been preserved by a local rancher. One of the soiled cards in the leather case advises that the makers are, "*Fabricantes de Naipes Superiores*". In those days a club was a club and a spade was a spade. The clubs on the cards are no flowery ornament but real clubs of the variety that Alley Oop uses.

Arrival of the "laws" from the Border had a good effect, however. The wiser bad men left for parts unknown without waiting to argue with the Rangers. Although the killings diminished after the coming of the Rangers, it was many years later, in fact only after the town had died, that the Texas Rangers were removed.

Tascosa began to decline when fencing of the western range stopped cattle trailing, and herds no longer went up the trail by way of Tascosa to Dodge City and Montana. The Ft. Worth and Denver Railway built through the Panhandle in 1887; and the town of Amarillo, 30 miles to the southeast, became a rival. The Santa Fe and the Pecos Valley railways also built into Amarillo, and the business that once went to where the cow trails crossed went to the town where the railroads crossed. Amarillo became the growing city that the founders of Tascosa had dreamed of.

The county seat was moved to Vega. The old courthouse became the property of Lee Bivins and was converted into a ranch house. The McCormicks stayed on, however, happy in their modest home. Mickie had been shot during the boom days at Silver City, New Mexico, and the wound continued to bother him. Death came in 1912. Although the McCormicks lived within 150 yards of the graveyard, the belle of old Tascosa did not intend that her beloved Mickie should be buried with the tough characters of Boot Hill. She took him down to a cemetery at the LIT ranch and laid him to rest among honorable pioneers.

A New Tascosa was built on the F. D. W. railway, but it did not flourish. When the author first visited old Tascosa in 1936 only two houses were still standing. One was the old courthouse, remodeled into a ranch house and the property of Julian Bivins of Amarillo. The other, the McCormick residence, lay in a tangle of plum bushes at the foot of Boot Hill. In the shade of its crumbling adobe walls sat an old lady dreaming of the days when she was the belle of old Tascosa. Calmly and unafraid, she was waiting to be laid to rest beside her beloved Mickie in the cemetery at the LIT ranch.

Chapter V

JOHN S. CHISUM AND HIS JINGLE BOBS

The General Behind the Guns in America's Greatest Cattle War.

"John S. Chisum was unquestionably the largest individual cattle owner in the United States and probably the greatest cattleman in the world," according to a history of the state of New Mexico.

Of him a publication of the American Historical Society says: "His life, if written in detail, would present a clear, correct, and forceful picture of pioneer times with various characters of frontier life with all its dangers, its privations, its horrors, its pleasures, and its prosperity."

Chisum's cattle watered on the Pecos River in New Mexico while grazing the western slope of the Staked Plains for 100 miles. Although generally regarded as a Pecos Valley cattleman, his activities so thoroughly included the "Llano Estacado" that the story of the Great Plateau would hardly be complete without a chapter about him.

This man that historians have called "Cattle King of America", and who was the general behind the guns in America's greatest cattle war, was born August 15, 1824, in Hardeman County, Tennessee, and came to Texas with his mother and step-father in 1837. His boyhood was spent on a farm in Red River Colony. His first real start in life was made when he acquired a tract of land and opened the townsite of Paris, Texas. He became a building contractor and erected the first courthouse at Paris when Lamar County was organized. Later he was elected County Clerk of that county and held the office eight years.

Chisum was about 30 years old when he began buying cattle from surrounding farms and selling them to local butchers. Then in 1854 he trailed a herd to Shreveport, Louisana. This was one of the first ever driven out of Texas, the cradle of the American cattle industry. Another man put up most of the money for the drove of 500 head that went to the adjoining state. Insects harassed the cattle on their way through the swamps. Mud balls and cockle burs accumulated on their tails, and the tails of some of the animals actually came off. Chisum lost money on this trip, but he gathered another small herd and drove them to Little Rock, Arkansas. He realized a small profit from this second undertaking but became convinced that little could be made from driving Texas cattle to the east on account of the insects, dense woods, and broad rivers.

He realized that Texas, especially the western part, was the natural home of the cow, for more wild cattle (buffalo) lived there than any place in the world. Tame cattle had been increasing rapidly since the days when they were introduced at the Spanish missions, but there was no market for them. Beef was high on the Atlantic seaboard, but there were no railroads to take the cattle to the East. Chisum believed, however, that he could eventually solve the market problem. In 1857 he went west and established a ranch in Denton County. Settlers were rapidly taking possession of the land. After six years in Denton County, Chisum pushed into the Comanche Indian country in West Texas and established a ranch on the Concho River near where San Angelo now stands. This was a prairie country with just enough broken land and timber to give protection to stock when blizzards swept down from the high, cold plateau of the Staked Plains. Most of the cattle that Chisum took to the Concho belonged to S. K. Fowler of New York and were being handled by Chisum for a share of the calf crop.

Chisum's ranch was exposed to raids of the Comanches from the Staked Plains and from Mexican bandits along the Rio Grande. He had been on the river only a few months when thieves came and drove off a lot of horses. Chisum and three companions set out in pursuit of the outlaws. They overtook the bandits at Horse Head crossing on the Pecos River. In the fight that followed, the ranchers killed three of the rustlers and recovered the stock.

In 1866, three years after Chisum established his ranch on the Concho, the United States government started building a fort on the river to protect the region. This military post was located where the stream forks, forming the North, South, and Middle Conchos. At first only a settlement, the town of San Angelo grew up under the protection of Ft. Concho.

The government became engaged in a series of Indian wars about 1864. In New Mexico, General J. H. Charleton and Col. Kit Carson were waging a vigorous campaign against the Navajos and Apaches. Much of New Mexico was a desert region with few buffalo to supply the soldiers with meat, so the government announced it would pay good prices for beef delivered to the armies in the Territory. Chisum decided to engage in the hazardous undertaking of supplying beef to armies in the field against the Indians.

By 1866 Carson had whipped the Navajos and was holding about 7,000 of that tribe prisoner at Ft. Sumner on the upper Pecos in New Mexico. The fort was on the river forming the western boundary of the Staked Plains. He had made less progress against the Apaches but had forced about 400 of that tribe to go to the reservation at Ft. Sumner. The government was having to feed both the soldiers and Indians at that place, and Chisum decided to drive a herd of steers from his ranch on the Concho in Texas to the fort on the Pecos in New Mexico. He would have to fight his way through a region infested with Comanches and Apaches, but he was willing to do this in order to secure a good price for his cattle.

Two other ranchers, Charles Goodnight and Oliver C. Loving of Palo Pinto, had already started driving cattle to the western forts. These two combined their herds and forces in order to have better protection from the Indains and started to Ft. Sumner with a party of 20 men. Chisum gathered 600 steers and set out for New Mexico soon after the Goodnight-Loving cattle went by on their way to the Pecos. There were only ten men in Chisum's party. This was more than enough to handle the small drove of steers but not enough to face the Indians. The high and almost waterless plateau of the Llano Estacado lay between Chisum's ranch on the Concho and Ft. Sumner. It not only had very little water but was the stronghold of the Comanches. Chisum, like Goodnight and Loving, decided it would be best to take a more circuitous route and avoid this plain. He proceeded up the Middle Concho toward the west, expecting to cross the divide to the Pecos and ford that stream.

Chisum's outfit saw signs of Indians soon after passing the place where the government was building Ft. Concho, but they reached the head of the Concho without encountering any Comanches. Between the head of this stream and the Pecos lay about 40 miles of desert. The cattle had to be driven almost day and night in crossing this. It was a guant and thirst crazed herd that reached the Pecos after three days without water, and crossed the stream at Horse Head crossing. This historic crossing had been the scene of many battles. It was here that Chisum and three companions, Frank Tanksley, Abe Hunter, and Robert K. Wiley had overtaken the bandit three years earlier with horses they had stolen from Chisum.

The Pecos had long been the dividing line between the Comanches on the east and the Apaches on the west. Although the valley of the Rio Grande River 100 miles farther west had been occupied for over 300 years by Spaniards and Mexicans, no one had ventured into the Pecos Valley until Ft. Sumner was built in 1862. Traveling about 10 miles a day, the Chisum herd turned north and ascended the Pecos for 300 miles without seeing a ranch until near Ft. Sumner. A chain of rugged mountains ran parallel with the river, their purple peaks rising against the sky far to the west. To the east of the Pecos lay the high plateau of the Llano Estacado or Staked Plains, home of the Kiowas, Comanches, and buffaloes. Except for an occasional cottonwood or hackberry, the Pecos Valley was treeless.

Six companies of soldiers were on duty at Ft. Sumner watching the Navajos and Apaches, trying to teach them to farm by diverting water from the Pecos for irrigation. The government was distributing 30,000 pounds of beef every day to the Indians. On reaching Ft. Sumner Chisum learned that the Comanches had wounded Oliver Loving while he was crossing the Pecos and that the cattleman had died soon after reaching the Fort.

The Concho River cattleman reached Ft. Sumner too late to sell his steers that year, but he under bid all competitors and got the contract to supply 7,000 head of cattle for the Indians in 1867. He sent his cattle to winter on the Pecos about 35 miles below the fort. The cow camp was pitched in a cottonwood grove on the banks of the river where there would be water and fuel. Mexicans had named this grove "Bosque Grande," which means big woods. Chisum made this his headquarters during his early trail driving operations and gradually converted it into a ranch. Bosque Grande became the first big cattle ranch in eastern New

Mexico. Here was grass and water without limit and without competition, except from Indians and buffaloes.

Chisum was too busy fullfilling his beef contract to bring in cattle to stock the range for a year or two, but by the end of 1872 he had 15,000 head at Bosque Grand. In 1868 the Apaches at Fort Sumner ran away and went on the warpath. The government sent the Navajos to a new reservation in northwestern New Mexico and northeastern Arizona, and Ft. Sumner was abandoned. Chisum got a contract to supply 1,700 head of cattle for Ft. Stanton in the Apache Indian country of New Mexico. He bought the cattle from a rancher on the South Concho and started to Ft. Stanton. When east of the Guadalupe Mountains about 200 miles from the fort, Indians in overwhelming numbers attacked his outfit, stampeeded the cattle, and made off with 1,165 head. The stock was never recovered. He had paid $18.00 per head for the steers and was to have received $35.00 a head.

When the Indians killed Oliver Loving, Goodnight was left without a partner. The Palo Pinto cattleman believed that he could make some money by trailing to Colorado. There were a lot of miners in that state who needed beef. There was also some demand for cows and heifers to stock new ranches. Goodnight proposed that Chisum join him in driving cattle to Colorado. They made an agreement whereby Chisum was to buy the cattle in Texas and bring them to Bosque Grande. Goodnight was to meet him there and trail the cattle to Colorado and sell them. They were to divide the profit and loss equally. Chisum and Goodnight drove cattle to the mountain state two years and cleared $35,000. Chisum's half of the profit went into cows and heifers to stock the range at Bosque Grande. Goodnight put his money into a ranch on the Arkansas River in Colorado.

Chisum's chief competitor for the beef contracts was a man named L. G. Murphy. Murphy had a ranch on the Carrizozo Plains about 100 miles west of Bosque Grande. He also had a trading post at the Mexican settlement "La Placita de la Bonita", in the Capitan Mountains.

This trading post later became the town of Lincoln and county seat of Lincoln County. Murphy became political boss of the new county, which included all of southeastern New Mexico. The Mescalero Apaches were rounded up in 1873 and put on a reservation in the White Mountains under the guns of Ft. Stanton. This left the lower Pecos free from their depredations, and Chisum decided to establish a ranch at South Spring River, a beautiful little stream that empties into the Pecos near where Roswell now stands. This was about 40 miles down the river from his Bosque Grande ranch. He also established a cow camp at Carlsbad Springs, 80 miles farther down the Pecos. Chisum brought cattle from his ranches in Texas and stocked the lower Pecos with 11,000 head. He now had 26,000 head of cattle in New Mexico, and this herd increased rapidly. He branded 9,231 cows in 1875 and judged that his cowboys had found and branded only three-fourths of those that belonged to him. The Jingle Bob cattle, as Chisum's was called, went up and down the Pecos, from Anton Chico to the Texas line, a range more than 150 miles long. It went out to the Staked Plains on the east and crossed the Rio Hondo and Penasco rivers to the mountains, 75 miles to the west. On this unlimited range, his 26,000 cattle soon grew into the largest herd in the United States.

L. G. Murphy, who heretofore had confined his ranching operations to the Carrizozo region, also took advantage of the freeing of the lower Pecos from the Apaches and established a ranch at Seven Rivers, a short distance above Chisum's cow camp at Carlsbad Springs. Thus these men who had been bitter rivals for the beef contract became competitors for control of the range on the lower Pecos. Murphy sent 3,000 cows and heifers to Seven Rivers. During the years that followed, he sold so many cattle from his ranch on the Pecos that people called his cattle "the magic herd." Chisum believed that many of these cattle were his mavericks that Murphy was capturing and branding faster than Chisum's cowboys could get them.

By 1877 Chisum had 70,000 or 80,000 head of cattle on the Pecos. Among these were 5,000 or 6,000 mavericks, or unbranded animals. Many cowboys and small ranchers soon built up large herds by putting their brand on these cattle that really belonged to Chisum. Some of these fellows, especially those in the mountains where concealment was easy, did not stop with branding mavericks. They stole large herds of Jingle Bob cattle and butchered them or sold them to distant ranches.

As Chisum's cattle increased, the number that white rustlers and Indians stole became enormous. On July 15, 1874, Indians made a raid on his ranch at Bosque Grande, stealing 150 head of horses and at the time taking 65 head that were about 12 miles up the river. White men stole 135 horses from the ranch at South Spring River the same year. The rustlers and Indians not only stole stock, they killed many of the cattlemen. Indians killed Jack Holt of the Roswell community in 1873 and the next year scalped Newt Higgins, the man who carried the mail from Roswell to Ft. Sumner. Many desperados came into New Mexico following the gold strikes at Elizabethtown and White Oaks. There was little law in the country, and many cases were tried before "Judge Lynch". A man who had committed murder was tried before this court of the range and hanged at Bosque Grande. Another who was found guilty of the same offense was shot at Navar's Bend on the Pecos.

Chisum sold 6,000 head of cattle to John P. Clum, Indian agent of the San Carlos Apaches in Arizona in 1876 and delivered them at Croton Springs, Arizona. In 1877 he trailed 6,000 choice steers to Ft. Dodge, Kansas. He also sold 4,000 "moss-horns" to the San Carlos Indian agent that year. While trailing the steers to Arizona, Chisum found some of his cattle on the Rio Grande near Dona Ana. Mexicans claimed the cattle and refused to give them up. The natives had either stolen the cattle or bought them from thieves. In the fight that resulted, Chisum's cowboys killed several of the Mexicans, taking the cattle by force.

Mescalero Apaches kept leaving their reservation in the White Mountains of New Mexico to steal cattle from Chisum on the Pecos. After enduring this for a while, Chisum followed a band of the Indians to the reservation, killed several of the Apaches, and drove his cattle home.

Then white thieves descended on Robert K. Wiley's camp, killed an employee named Yopp, and drove off 400 head of cattle belonging to Chisum and Wiley, his associate. Chisum found that some of Murphy's men had been at the camp and suspected that they had stolen the cattle. The Murphy men said they went to the camp while trailing thieves.

Chisum soon surpassed Murphy as a cattleman; but this Texan, who had been a good politician himself, was no match for the mountain cattleman when it came to dirty politics. Murphy was political boss of Lincoln County and elected whom he pleased. Chisum's attorney, Alexander McSwain, soon got in bad by operating a store in competition with Murphy's firm. Then, to make the situation worse, Chisum opened a bank in Lincoln that began to take business that had formerly gone to Murphy's bank. An Englishman, John H. Tunstall, who operated a ranch on the Felix River, joined Chisum in the banking business and became vice-president of the institution. McSwain was made cashier of the bank, while Chisum was the president.

With all this competition, trouble was almost inevitable. Sheriff William Brady ignored the new banking instution and deposited all tax money in the bank of his political boss, Murphy. Tunstall criticized the sheriff and Murphy's bank. Thus Chisum, Tunstall, and McSwain soon found themselves arrayed against Murphy and Brady.

Murphy had never been considered scrupulous in his methods by some people, and he now began to fight the cattle king of the Pecos and his associates with any means available. He took two influential young men, J. J. Dolan and John Riley, into his business and prepared to destroy his competitor if possible.

Riley's father-in-law, Col. Amily Fritz, died leaving a $10,000 life insurance policy; and the heirs employed McSwain to collect the insurance for them. McSwain succeeded in collecting the amount after a trip to New York and other difficulties. When the time came for settlement, a dispute arose as to the expense and attorney fees. This gave Murphy, Dolan, and Riley the opportunity they had wanted. They induced the heirs to attach the McSwain store. Sheriff Brady served the papers, and padlocked the store, just what the Murphy mercantile firm wanted. Not satisfied with closing the rival business house, an attachment was taken out on the Tunstall ranch on the ground that Tunstall was McSwain's partner.

Sheriff Brady sent Bill Morton, foreman of the Murphy ranch, and a strong force of cowboys to take charge of the Tunstall ranch. The men not only took possession of the ranch under the attachment but killed the owner. Morton's men excused themselves by saying the Englishman had tried to run off with the saddle horses. Two of Tunstall's employees, however, said the banker had only eight horses in his possession and that he was shot while holding his hands over his head.

Chisum and McSwain got a warrant for Morton for the murder of their partner. Sheriff Brady showed little inclinatio to act against the foreman of Murphy's ranch, so the Tunstall and Chisum cowboys went after him. They captured Morton and Frank Baker, who had taken part in the killing of Tunstall, and shot them. A man named McCloskey tried to interfere with the execution and was killed by Frank McNabb, one of Chisum's men.

A short time after the execution of Morton, the enraged Tunstall cowboys, led by Billy the Kid, boldly rode into Lincoln and shot it out with Sheriff Brady and his deputies. Brady and Deputy George Heinman were killed. Billy the Kid was wounded.

Governor Axtell appointed another Murphy man, George W. Peppin, as sheriff, and the war went on. Peppin started to Lincoln with about 30 men. When 4 or 5 miles from the county seat, they met Frank McNabb and two companions, Frank Coe and Ab Saunders, of the Chisum ranch and opened fire upon them. Saunders fell at the first volley. McNabb took to the hills but was surrounded and killed. Coe had almost passed out of shooting range when a bullet from a buffalo gun killed his horse. He surrendered and was taken to Lincoln.

McSwain had posted watchmen around his residence and the Chisum bank to prevent the buildings from being burned or dynamited by the Murphy faction. Urged on by his political boss, Peppin decided to disarm the McSwain party. The lawyer told the sheriff there was no law against a man protecting his property and warned Brady and the Murphy cowboys to keep off his premises.

Peppin appealed to Col. N. A. Dudley, commander of Ft. Stanton, for aid, and attacked the McSwain party with

60 men. Chisum's attorney and 14 followers barricaded themselves in the McSwain dwelling. Bob Beckwith and John McKinney, two of the Murphy and Peppin faction, were killed in the seige. Harvey Morris and Francisco Senora, two of the defenders, were also slain. The Murphy and Peppin men set fire to the roof of the house. The adobe walls would not burn, however; and the McSwain party managed to hold out until night. Outnumbered and fearing the building would be dynamited, the besieged men decided to abandon the dwelling. McSwain and Billy the Kid remained until the last and kept up a brisk fire while the others crawled away in the darkness or made their way out by sudden dashes. One of the fleeing men, Vincente Romero, was shot down but managed to crawl away and survived. As the fire from the house subsided, Sheriff Peppin and J. J. Dolan of the Murphy firm led a general assault. McSwain was killed in the final charge, but Billy the Kid escaped.

Chisum had now lost his banking partner, his attorney, and several cowboys. Mrs. McSwain employed Houston J. Chapman as her attorney, and the Murphy faction promptly killed him. Death for Chisum appeared to be only a matter of time.

At this critical stage, President Hayes took a hand in affairs. He recalled Governor Axtell and appointed General Lew Wallace governor of New Mexico. Governor Wallace took prompt and impartial steps to end the great cattle war. He called in the leaders and heard both sides of the trouble. He then issued a proclamation of amnesty to all except Billy the Kid, J. J. Dolan, and Col. Dudley.

The commander of Ft. Stanton faced the inquiry into his conduct, and lost his command. Dolan, Murphy's partner, was tried for the killing of Chapman and was acquitted. Billy the Kid was afraid to stand trial, and he became an outlaw. The cowboy was killed two years later at Ft. Sumner after having killed 21 men, a man for every year of his short life.

During his last years, Chisum began irrigating a large area along South Spring River by diverting water from the beautiful little stream. Alfalfa and oats were planted for wintering saddle horses. The first trees of a 600 acre apple orchard were set out. The ranch at South Spring River became one of the most beautiful in New Mexico. Settlers came and turned the neighboring streams, North Spring River and the Berrendo, into irrigation ditches. Artesian water was discovered later, and today the largest artesian wells in the world help to irrigate what was once the Chisum range.

In time, other cow outfits crowded in on the Pecos; and the "Cattle King of America" was compelled to reduce his herds. The great cattleman died December 23, 1884, at Eureka Springs, Arkansas, leaving a half million dollars worth of cattle on the range. His body was taken back to Texas and buried at Paris, the town he had founded.

Col. C. C. Slaughter, owner of a million acres of land and the largest taxpayer in the state of Texas. Son of a cattleman-preacher, he used his first earnings to buy cattle instead of a saddle. Making his home in Dallas when not at the Long-S ranches, he became an outstanding civic leader and philanthropist before his death in 1919. (Picture courtesy of Mrs. John Dean, daughter of Col. Slaughter.)

In April of 1888 this beautiful capitol building was completed in Austin, Texas by the Capitol Land Syndicate. In 1885 the state of Texas deeded 3,000,000 acres of land to the Syndicate in payment for erection of this building. The land became the XIT Ranch.

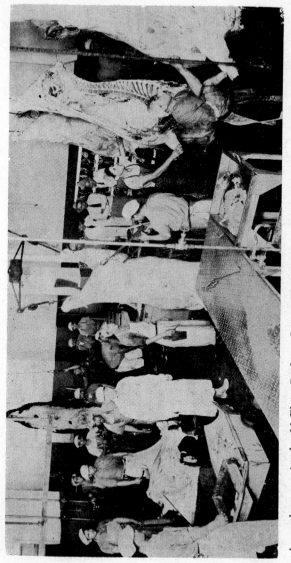

An early scene in the McElroy Packing Co. at El Paso. John T. McElroy solved his marketing problem by opening the packing company in 1919 for the slaughtering and processing of his own herd. Ed R. Ardoin, Jr. was a partner in the company.

A typical scene of a herd on the trail in the Pecos River country near Carlsbad, New Mexico.

Around Up Scene on the Range

Cowboys brand a calf on the Quitaque Division of the Slaughter ranches in the rough country along the eastern edge of the Cap Rock.

Chapter VI.

CLIFFORD B. JONES OF THE SPUR OUTFIT

The Cowboy Who Became a College President

The 439,972 acre Spur ranch had its beginning in 1878 when Jim Hall brought 1,900 head of cattle from the Gulf Coast below Goliad and turned them loose in the fertile valleys and broad mesas up along the Caprock in West Texas.

The site selected for the ranch was just under the Caprock where the cattle could go out on the broad prairie of the Staked Plains in summer and retire below the sheltering cliffs of the "Cap" when blizzards swept across the great open plains. A more ideal location could hardly have been found. Canyon Blanco, where the longhorns were turned loose, had been a favorite range of the buffalo; and the surrounding country proved to be just as satisfactory for the tame cattle.

Headquarters for the Spur outfit were established in the vicinity of Soldiers Mound, which had been the supply base for Gen. Ronald S. Mackenzie's army during its campaigns of 1871-2 and 1874-5 against the Comanches. Soldiers Mound had been fortified and protected by Major (later Major General) Thomas M. Anderson, 10th U. S. Infantry, and his battalion, composed of Companies A. C. I. and K.

Capt. R. G. Carter, last survivor of the Fourth United States Cavalry, who helped to rid the Staked Plains of the Indians, told the following story in an interview:

Our camps for the years 1871, 1872, 1874, and 1875 were at various times on the Freshwater Fork of the Brazos, on Duck Creek, Double Mountain Fork of the Brazos, near the mouth of McClellan's Creek, and numerous other places.

We scouted out from our base at Soldiers Mound, which was supplied from Ft. Griffin by wagon trains and pack mules that went as far west as Ft. Sumner and Bucom, New Mexico. Major T. M. Anderson, 10th U. S. Infantry (later major general in command of the first expedition to the Philippines) commanded the supply camp in 1874-5. It was called Anderson's Fort. It was guarded by several companies of the 10th and 11th infantry. Anderson, to make himself secure from attack in the rear by any large band of Indians that might surprise us, piled up boxes, barrels, logs, etc., in a great rectangle. Hence Anderson's Fort.

Some of our men died there or near there and were probably buried in the mound. The man I lost was named Gregg. We buried him at the southwest slope of the butte at the mouth of Canyon Blanco near where Quanah shot him out of the saddle. The chief used him as a shield as we, a small party, fell back. Otherwise, I could have killed Quanah myself, as I was only 30 or 40 yards from him.

But there were too many of the Indians for me to handle, and we were fighting a waiting battle until the main command should come over the hills from the Freshwater Fork to our rescue. When they did come, the Indians fled up the Canyon and later out onto the Staked Plains.

All of our action took place at or near Blanco, Tule, and Palo Duro canyons and Red River near the mouth of McClellan Creek. In 1872 we captured 1,300 squaws and children and 800 ponies. The Indians recovered the horses; and we shot the next ponies we captured-2,200 head.

Mackenzie had vanquished Quanah when Hall arrived with his Spur cattle, although there were still some scattered bands of Indians in the country. The stockman was so well pleased with his ranch location that he sent to New Mexico for his share of the Cross-L cattle on the Cimarron and added these to the Spur outfit. The Cross-L stock belonged to the three Hall brothers, Jim, Nathan, and William.

The cattle from South Texas were infected with fever ticks; and the fever spread rapidly through the Cross-L herd, almost wiping out these cattle that had built up no resistance to the disease. The parasites did not thrive in the high, dry altitude of the Caprock though, and the disease was eradicated. As long as no infection was imported from the lowlands, the Spur cattle flourished. Today tick fever is unknown on the Staked Plains.

Stephens and Harris bought the Hall cattle and Spur brand in 1882. During this early period, the Spur cattle grazed the free range. Texas, however, adopted a policy of giving large tracts to railway companies in an effort to stimulate the building of new lines; and alternating sections of the Spur range soon passed into the hands of the H. & G. N. R. R.

Britton and Lomax bought out Stephens and Harris in the early eighties and founded the Espuela Land and Cattle Co., "espuela" being the Spanish word for Spur. They began to buy railroad lands and, when possible, the intervening sections taken up by settlers. Lomax selected the beautiful Spur headquarters about 1883. The springs and lovely natural scenery surrounding the Headquarters make it one of the most beautiful in West Texas. It is 9 miles northwest of the present town of Spur.

Retaining an interest, the owners sold to a Scotch syndicate; and the word "Limited" was added to the title. Lomax continued to manage the ranch.

Among the cowboys who worked for the Spur in its early period were Jake Raines and Jeff D. Harkey. Harkey came up from the Gulf coast with the cattle that Hall bought from Refugio County. He liked the country so well that he stayed with the Spur outfit for many years, and remained in the county after he retired.

Raines came from New Mexico with the Cross-L Hall stock and spent over 30 years on the Spur ranch. The ranch changed hands five times, but Raines was always retained by the new owners. He was a line rider after barbwire enclosed the Spur range. He held nearly every job on the big ranch and eventually became an authority on cattle brands of the Southwest.

There is a story, probably fictitious, that he had the Spur brand tatooed on his left hip and wore his hair long to conceal the underslope of his left ear. His more than thirty years in the saddle for one cow outfit unquestionably made him the top hand of this great ranch.

Fred Horsbrugh became manager of the ranch in 1889 and continued the policy of expansion until the company owned 673 sections in Dickens, Garza, Kent, and Crosby counties, a large per cent of which was suitable for farming purposes. Henry Johnstone became manager in 1904 and held that position until 1907.

In 1906 the Spur ranch came to the attention of S. M. Swenson and Son, and negotiations were begun for the purchase of the property with the idea of selling the more level portion to northern and eastern farmers for agricultural purposes. The Swensons were one af the oldest and wealthiest families of Texas and already owned large ranches in Throckmorton, Jones, Motley, Cottle, King, Stonewall, and Haskell counties.

S. M. Swenson, native of Sweden and founder of the family in America, came to Texas about 1835 and began his career as a merchant and banker at Austin. As a man of large means, he helped to finance Houston's army during the Texas Revolution and is said to have played much the same part in winning the independence of Texas as Robert Morris played in financing the American Revolution.

After the Republic of Texas was founded, it was S. M. Swenson who introduced the six-shooter into the Ranger forces. The slow loading single shot pistols and rifles of the Texans were little better than the faster but less effective bows and arrows of the Indians, but the six-shooter gave the Rangers a half dozen shots without pausing to load.

A short time after the introduction of this weapon, an Indian chief explained his defeat by saying, "Pale-face fire one shot with his gun and six with his butcher knife."

Although the head offices of S. M. Swenson and Sons were moved to New York City, E. P. Swenson, senior partner of the firm, and S. A. Swenson, who died in 1927, were both born in Austin.

Although the Swensons were big cow men, and their S M S ranch near Stamford, Texas, was one of the largest in the country, they made early plans for selling the better part of the Spur land for farming purposes. During the first six months following the opening of the ranch for settlement, 16,000 head of cattle were removed to make room for the farmers. In 1910, another 17,000 were sold to vacate more land. There is still considerable stock on the rougher portions of the ranch, but farmers have been gradually crowding out the cattle ever since S. M. Swenson and Sons took charge of the ranch February 20, 1907.

Charles Adam Jones, who had been general purchasing agent for the Armour Packing Co. in Kansas City, became manager of the Spur ranch for S. M. Swenson and Sons and held that position until 1913, when he went to Freeport, Texas, to look after the sulphur interest of the Swensons. He was later transferred to the head of the company in New York. When Mr. Jones gave up the management of the Spur ranch, he was succeeded by his son, Clifford B. Jones.

Clifford B. Jones distinguished himself as a cattleman, a banker, and an educator. He was manager of the Spur ranch for more than 20 years, became president of the Spur Security Bank, and finally president of Texas Technological College at Lubbock. In tracing the history of the Spur ranch, no better authority could be found than this versatile leader who managed the great ranch for two decades early in his career. In describing the *Espuela* ranch and its surroundings, Mr. Jones writes the following account.

Although John Arrowsmith's map of Texas, published in London in 1841, shows this section of Texas to have been explored by LeGrand in 1833, probably the first reconnoisance of any note was by Capt. R. B. Marcy, U. S. Army, who in the summer of 1854 led an expedition from Fort Smith, Ark., into West Texas. It is known that this wagon train crossed Garza county, and it is presumed he crossed the lands that later became the Spur ranch.

Daniel Webster's fallacious judgment of the value of the so-called Louisiana Purchase was fully equalled by Capt. Marcy's report on this immediate section. Marcy says, "Those wilds are totally unfit. Destitute of everything that can sustain or make life tolerable, they must remain as they are, uninhabitated and unhabitable."

Cheffin's map of the Republic of Texas, published in Southampton, England, shows what is now Dickens county and the Spur ranch as lying within John Cameron's Grant, and as occupied by Comanche Indians, droves of wild cattle and horses.

It is interesting to realize that the Spur ranch was once in the edge of the sea. Shells and the remains of prehistoric reptiles known to inhabit the marshes and edge of salt water are frequently found. In 1920 Prof. E. C. Case, Paleontologist for the University of Michigan, found near Spur a prehistoric reptile hitherto unknown to the scientific world. He named the animal 'Desmatosuchus Spurensis' after the Spur ranch on which it was found. The reptile was 18 feet long and in a remarkable good state of preservation. A splendid picture of this petrified giant reptile is available, showing a form of life which inhabited this section millions of years prior to the Mastadon age. Remains of the Mastadon, much larger than elephants, have been found on the Spur ranch.

It is interesting, also, to realize that eons later this country was above the Caprock and on the Staked Plains. Scientist say that the Caprock was once far east and south of its present location, and that during a period of untold centuries the processes of erosion have pushed it continuously backward.

Worthy of note, too, is the evidence found here that during eruptions of volcanoes in what is now Colorado and New Mexico, this section was covered to shallow depths by volcanic ash, millions of tons of which are found today near Spur. Dr. Udden thinks the Spanish Peaks of Colorado a likely source, as well as Mt. Capulin in New Mexico.

Then in the natural order of things came the great herds of buffalo, and antelope, deer, bears, panthers, lobo wolves, prairie chickens, and wild turkeys. The scene of the best story ever written of the extermination of the buffalo, "The Thundering Herd," by Zane Grey, was laid here. Pease River just north of us is particularly mentioned.

Dickens County is named for John Dickens, one of those who fought at the Alamo. This county was organized March 19,1891. Prior to that time it was successively attached to Mitchell and Baylor counties for judicial purposes. After the organization of Crosby County, Dickens County was attached to it. I once asked an old-timer to what was Dickens County attached for judicial purpose before being attached to Mitchell; and with a significant look he replied, 'We didn't know or care much about judicial purposes in those days.'

The first county officials were:
County Judge, A. J. McClain; County Attorney, John A. Gren; County Treasurer, J. M. Jones; County Clerk, Sid Dunwoody; Sheriff, J. D. Harkey; Tax Assessor, J. D. Kutch; County Surveyor, John Hale.

Hon. B. G. Worswick early succeeded to the County Attorneyship, and it is a striking tribute to him that he undoubtedly has the record of the longest continuous service as county attorney of any county attorney in the state.

The first district judge was Hon. W. R. McGill. The first district attorney was W. Q. Henderson, who was succeeded by Judge Kinder, now of Plainview.

According to W. R. Stafford, who came here from Wharton County, Texas, in 1883, the first cattle brought to this immediate section were the "Jingle Bobs". They were brought by Coggins & Collison from the Chisum ranch on the Pecos in 1877.

In the early days the two largest herds were those of the Spurs and the Matadors, the former owned successively by the Espuela Cattle Co. of Fort Worth, and the Espuela Land and Cattle Company, Ltd., of London, from whom in 1907 S. M. Swenson & Sons and associates acquired the Spur ranch. The Espuela Company's diary of November 30, 1886, shows a total of 52,986 head of cattle on the Spur ranch, of which 20,346 were cows. The Spur herd had its basis in the old Cross-L brought in August, 1878, from the New Mexico-Colorado line by Jim Hall. Jeff Harkey, who later became sheriff of Dickens county, came with these cattle. The Matador herd had its origin in the 50 brand cattle brought from Ellis County. The Matador company branded a number of buffalo with the T-41, their early brand on the left side.

The early history of the country was the history of the cattle industry. To those early pioneers, and especially to the women of those days who bore with such fortitude the hardships, privations, and dangers of frontier life, a loving appreciative tribute is due.

Cattle in those days were frequently finished in the Northwest and moved from here usually as 2-year olds, along the old Chisholm Trail, via Amarillo to Colorado, Wyoming, Montana, and the Dakotas. The trail herd comprised several thousand head. Completion of the main line of the Ft. Worth and Denver in 1888 permitted shipment by rail.

The first drift fence in Dickens County was built by the Spur in 1884. The drift fence of the Llano Cattle Company in Garza County was built in 1882. These fences, and that of Col. Goodnight, who ran the F and JA brands near the main line of the Denver, were the only ones between Colorado City, Texas, and Ft. Dodge Kansas, according to the best information obtainable.

Probably the last buffalo killed on the Spur ranch was in August, 1883, at about the location of what afterwards became the town of Espuela. The buffalo was shot by a boy known as Billy, who worked for the Triangle outfit.

According to W. L. Hyatt, the Causey boys were among the first to hunt buffalo on the Spur ranch. They, and Moore, and Grill, and Patton found the hunting excellent here and appear to have killed most of the buffalo grazing this section. They hauled the hides to Ft. Griffin. The only time that "Uncle Bill" Hyatt ever cut his rope off anything was when he roped a buffalo bull near here during the roundup of 1883.

W. C. Docum, who came here in the middle seventies, and S. T. Pepper, who came from Stephens County in 1877, were also among the buffalo hunters. Docum Creek was named after W. C. Docum, and one of the earliest post-offices in this section was known as Docum postoffice. Mail came up from Colorado City and went to Mt. Blanco by way of Docum.

That was before my time, but Bill Hyatt says, 'The whole surface of the country was covered with mustang horses and antelope. When the cattlemen came, they killed the mustangs to save the grass for cattle. The horses were of no value. They were too small and hard to tame - all mane and tail.'

'If early reports are correct,' Hyatt continued, 'the creeks and canyons along the eastern slope of the Caprock were full of turkeys. You just picked them off the limb of these cottonwoods. And quail - millions of them! Later hauled them out of here - killed them and trapped them. I have seen wagon loads after wagon loads; and turkeys, too, being hauled to market. And there were lots of rattlesnakes and vinegaroons. Not much hopes in those days for anything bitten by a vinegaroon. That grave along the fence about a mile northwest of the old Spur Headquarters is that of a nephew of A. T. (Bud) Campbell, who was bitten by a skunk. There were bears all over this country - in Croton

Breaks along Duck creek. Black bears mostly, and panther - you would often hear them scream. Many deer were in the shinnery.'

It is possible that the last Indian depredation in this immediate section was in 1883. The Comanches stole Sam Gholston's horses, and those of John and Bill Slaughter, including those named Sugar Child, Old Sorghum, and Taller Eye.

The last Indian fight of any moment near here was Gen. MacKenzie's engagement on the Tule, following which his troops killed hundreds of captured Indian horses.

The well-known MacKenzie Trail crossed the town of Spur at about the northeast corner of the Spur Inn. Just west of the town of Spur it branched, one trail going north along the ridge east of the Spur Ranch Headquarters to the Plains, climbing the Caprock south of the present Spur-Dickens-Crosbyton road and north of the head of Cottonwood.

The last person here captured by the Indians was Lee Parish, about 15 years old, in the summer of 1882 or 1883. Chat Dockum, who was with the Parish boy, outrode the Indians, who evidently fearful of trouble, released the Parish boy after keeping him for some time. They retained his horse and saddle. The Indians were Comanches, with the exception of one red-headed Indian, apparently a white child that had been stolen and reared by the Comanches. The capture occured on the plains a short distance from the present location of the Spur-Dickens-Crosbyton road.

Soldier's Mound has been referred to as the scene of the last Indian fight on the Spur range. It is known that General MacKenzie built a fort on the west side of the mound, and it is probable the name is taken from that association. There are several unmarked graves of soldiers on top of the mound, but whether they were killed in battles there or in fights elsewhere and brought to the fort for burial is not definitely known.

It was in 1907, when in London, that E. P. Swenson bought the Spur ranch for his firm, S. M. Swenson & Sons, and associates. The ranch consisted of 439,972 acres lying in Dickens, Kent, Crosby, and Garza counties. At that time, the ranch was devoted solely to the raising of cattle and sheep.

The Swensons soon began subdividing the more level portions of the ranch. The Swenson Company, with C. W. Post of Post City and Cooney & Bassett of Crosbyton, were the first in West Texas to offer land from the large ranches for sale to homeseekers in small tracts. Up until this time many of the ranches had been steadily increasing in size. The colonization project was a new policy that recognized the demand for farms and forecast the ultimate intensive development of the country.

Company records indicate that the first sale was made in August, 1908, to L. M. Hamilton of Orange, California. The town of Dickens, or a site near there, was under serious consideration by the Swenson Company as the principal town on the Spur ranch. On the other hand, engineers for the Burlington railroad had chosen a site several miles from the present town of Spur. The final location was agreed on at a conference between C. A. Jones, the manager for the Swensons, and Daniel Willard, executive head of the Burlington Railroad. Mr. Willard agreed to the site selected by Mr. Jones, who had recognized the natural advantages of beauty, drainage, proximity to abundant water, and large supply of gravel and sand. It is interesting to note that a large band of antelope were grazing on the site of Spur the day Mr. Jones drove over that part of the ranch seeking the best available location for the new town.

The first train of the Stamford & Northwestern Railway pulled into Spur November 1, 1909. The town was incorporated February 1, 1911. The first city officials were:

Geo. S. Link, mayor; W. G. Sherrod, commissioner; E. C. Edmonds, commissioner; Oscar Jackson, recorder and secretary; B. D. Glasgow, city attorney; Dr. J. E. Morris, health officer; J. M. Neeley, Marshal.

The streets of Spur were named after officials of the Ft. Worth & Denver and Burlington railways. Hill Street and Hill Heights were named for James Hill, president of the Great Northern and closely identified with the Burlington.

On the day of the formal opening of Spur, November 1, 1909, an average of one lot per minute was sold during the greater part of the day, selections previously having been made by the purchasers.

The first store opened at Spur was the Spur Hardware & Furniture Co., of which N. A. Baker was then active head.

The Spur Inn opened its doors September 3, 1910. The well-known author and war correspondent for the Saturday Evening Post, George Pattullo, then of Boston, was the first person to register. Pattullo later spent many months at Spur and at the Spur Ranch Headquarters, and wrote many of his Western stories here.

Many other authors and painters of note found inspiration and material on the Spur ranch. In addition to Pattullo, there were Emerson Hough; B. M. Bower; Frank Tenney Johnson (the painter); John Lomax, who has preserved cowboy songs for future generations; Freeman Tilden of the Country Gentlemen; Professor Crosby of the Massachusetts Institute of Technology; Prof. E. C. Case of the University of Michigan; Dr. J. A. Udden of the University of Texas; and many others.

The boring of the deep well at Spur, 4489 feet, the deepest in Texas at the time, was the inspiration of the present potash investigation in West Texas. A brine having a high potash content was found in that well at 2,000 feet.

Upon acquiring the Spur ranch, the Swenson Company undertook to rid the property of the prairie dogs. The company spent more than $70,000 in its campaign against this pest which feeds upon both crops and the range and succeeded in completely freeing the Spur lands of the rodents. Two complete outfits with chuck wagons and men and boys covered the 439,972 acre ranch three times, twice with poison grain and once with carbon bisulphide.

During the early days when this and adjoining counties paid bounties on prairie dog scalps the old Espuela Land & Cattle Co. was able to pay its taxes with prairie dog scalps, and at times left the counties in its debt.

The first airplane flight at Spur was made by Charles Theodore, employed by the Dickens County Fair Association to make exhibition flights during the Fair of September,

1916. His ship was of the Curtis biplane type, with the propeller at the back instead of at the front of the machine. There was no cockpit, and the pilot sat precariously strapped to on open seat attached to the rods which supported the forward landing wheel. He made several successful flights, but at each landing crashed into the Fair ground fences, owing to inability to shut off the engine. Later he was killed while stunt flying in Dallas.

S. M. Swenson & Sons brought the largely undeveloped region of the Spur ranch to the attention of officials of the Colorado & Southern Railway, with the result that the Wichita Valley line was extended to the center of the Spur lands; and plans begun to open the property for settlement. The formal opening of the new town of Spur, terminus of the railroad, was held November 1, 1909.

The Texas Spur, published by Oran McClure, on November 12, 1909, reports the opening of the Spur ranch for sale and settlement as follows:

At last the hundreds of people who have been waiting for the opening of Spur have been gratified, and the building of a modern city has begun and is being rapidly pushed. Monday, November 1, between 8:00 and 9:00 o'clock lots were placed on sale to the general public in Spur. The sale was conducted in front of the townsite office, where several hundred prospective buyers had congregated.

Chas. A. Jones, manager for S. M. Swenson & Sons, opened the sale by making a short talk, explaining the plan of sale and stating that a few lots had already been sold prior to the opening in order to establish solid and substantial business concerns, that some had been reserved for public institutions, but that no lots had been disposed of for speculative purposes and that it was the desire and intention to prevent as far as possible all speculation in the sale of the lots to the general public.

The sale of the business lots was turned over to Mr. Berthelot, and the residence property sales turned over to Mr. Andrew Swenson. These gentlemen checked off the lots selected and gave the purchaser a ticket to be presented to the office management where the sale would be ratified and the deeds drawn up.

When the word was given for the sale to begin, a veritable Oklahoma rush was made on the salesmen; and within a very short time every lot, both business and residence, within the townsite had been checked and sold to anxious purchasers. During the next two or three days the townsite office was crowded from morning to night ratifying the sales.

Immediately after the sale had been completed, a rush was made on lumbermen and carpenters; and the erection of temporary residences and buisness houses was soon under way.

Contrary to the desire and expectation of the townsite management in the sale of the lots, there was considerable speculation immediately after the sale closed. Those who were not large enough and disposed to crowd in and secure lots before they were all gone unhesitatingly paid premiums to those who were more fortunate in securing a nice selection of property, and in some instances several hundred dollars was made by individuals who secured first choice.

Today there are forty or more business houses already completed or under construction, including six lumber yards, three dry goods department stores, two grain and feed stores, a coal store, one drug store, three barber shops, three restaurants, one blacksmith shop, three or four land offices, two stables, a pool hall, postoffice, telephone exchange, school house, hotel, tin shop, depot, and meat market.

In the residence section of the town there are possibly thirty more houses under construction and other waiting for lumber, workmen, and other necessaries.

Drilling on the artesian well is progressing rapidly, and it is said that the management has made the statement that they will go the limit and then 10 feet deeper or secure artesian water. Of this we are assured, that Spur will be supplied with an abundance of good, pure water. If not from the well, other sources will be employed to supply the demand.

No town has ever been created and established under more favorable conditions and circumstances than Spur, and no town has a bigger territory from which to draw trade.

Spur has the very brightest future and will grow rapidly and become within a few years one of the most prominent commercial centers of Western Texas.

The surrounding country is at present undeveloped but rich in agricultural resources, and those who know say that the management of the Spur Farm Lands will advertise extensively in the north and east and bring the people here who will develop the country at once. It takes farms and farmers to make a town and country prosperous; and in seeking a location, the homeseeker cannot find a better and more productive agricultural section than the country surrounding Spur. The little farming that has heretofore been done in this section demonstrates this fact beyond a doubt.

A number of farms have already been sold, and preparations for making a crop are now being made by those who have bought land. Within the course of a few months we expect to see hundreds of new farm homes going up in every section of the country surrounding Spur.

As has been said heretofore, Spur and the Spur country has the most promising prospects and the very brightest future; and all who are here now are working together for the upbuilding of the town, development of the country, and the general prosperity of the people.

Settlement of the great ranch, which covered a large part of four counties, is still going on. Some of the land is too rough for cultivation and will always be used for ranching purposes. Clifford B. Jones was manager of the Spur lands for S. M. Swenson & Sons at the time the author gathered the material for this chapter. Doc Ellis was foreman of the cow ranch.

Clifford B. Jones not only made a reputation as one of the great cattlemen of the West but distinguished himself as a banker and educator. When Texas Technological College was established at Lubbock, Mr Jones was made chairman of the board of regents. Then came the depression years of the '30ies, and a move was started by certain "efficiency experts" to have the school broken up and its various departments

consolidated with other state colleges. Mr. Jones opposed
the movement, and took the college, as well as his bank and
the Spur ranch, safely through the trying years. When the
first president died, Mr. Jones was elected president of
Texas Technological College. Today, Texas Tech, with a
1,000 acre campus and buildings unsurpassed in size and
beauty, is a living monument to a cattleman who believed in
education. Thus we see that the cowboys who rode the
Staked Plains sometimes became bankers and college presi-
dents as well as stockmen, rodeo performers, and two-gun
men.

CHAPTER VII.

MAJ. GEORGE W. LITTLEFIELD
AND HIS YELLOW HOUSE RANCH

The Texas Ranger Who Made $6,000,000 in Ranching

Near its center the vast plateau of the Staked Plains is cut by a canyon several hundred feet deep and a mile wide. This ancient river bed is now dry except for some potash lakes and a few water holes that form in time of rain. About 40 miles west of Lubbock, Texas, a clear spring once gushed from the foot of a 100 foot cliff on this canyon and furnished the only wholesome water on that part of the plains.

In the white and yellow rocks of the canyon were many caves. In some of these prehistoric people once made their homes and slew the animals that came to drink at the spring. Following the cave men came the Comanches, who pitched their tepees in the canyon, and mounted on swift ponies and armed with bows and arrows, hunted the antelope and buffalo that watered at the spring. Spanish explorers, finding that some of the yellow caves had been inhabited, named the old river bed *el Canyon de las Casas Amarillos,* or "the canyon of the yellow houses."

The vast levels of the Staked Plains remained the home of the Comanches until 1875. From this high plateau they descended into central Texas to scalp the pale-face and to steal horses. Many an Indian brave went on a raid below the Caprock and came back famous as a warrior and rich in horses, or did not come back at all. The struggle between the whites in the lowlands and the red men on the plains went on with varying fortunes, while the Comanches fought first the Spaniards, then the Mexicans, later the Republic of Texas, and finally the United States. Once white men came to the canyon and on a peninsula that juts out into the valley above the spring built a crude fort of stones. This barricade was in the form of a half circle and blocked approach to the peninsula from the plains. The perpendicular walls of the peninsula gave protection on three sides. From the heights, the new comers could look out over the valley for miles and see foes or game that approached the spring. Neither Indian nor buffalo could approach the only drinking water in that part of the country without exposing themselves to the guns of the whites.

But the bold Comanches came stealthily during the night and attacked the men in their stronghold. Little is known of the fight, but it must have been long and fierce, for the area around the crude fort was filled with arrows and even today is a storehouse filled with arrow heads.

After Texas was annexed to the United States, the brave Comanches had a stronger foe than the Spaniards, Mexicans, and Texans had been. After numerous wars and broken peace treaties, the United States sent three armies against the Indians of the Llano Estacado. Col. Nelson A. Miles went south from Ft. Dodge, Kansas, striking from the north. Gen. Ronald S. Mackenzie advanced from Ft. Concho, Texas, and attacked the Indians on the east. Another army from Ft. Union, New Mexico, struck at the Comanches from the west. The Indians were caught between the three armies and finally were defeated in the winter of 1874. They were compelled to give up their homeland on the plains and go to a reservation in Oklahoma.

Then when buffalo became scarce below the Caprock in Texas, three hunters from Ft. Griffin went to the Staked Plains and pitched their camp at the spring in the *Canyon de las Casas Amarillos*. They translated the name and the place became Yellow House Canyon. These hunters, George and John Causey and Frank Lloyd, killed over 7,000 buffalo in Yellow House Canyon and Running Water draw in 1877. The wild cattle were killed for their hides. These were freighted to Ft. Griffin, over 200 miles to the east, and sold. The hunters received approximately $1.00 for each buffalo cow hide and $2.00 for the bull hides. The Causey brothers built an adobe house at the spring on Yellow House Canyon in 1879. This was the first house on what is now called the South Plains. In 1881 a mail route was laid out across the Llano Estacado from Colorado, Texas, to Ft. Sumner, New Mexico. This route ran by the Yellow House camp.

The buffalo were gone by 1882, and the hunters sold the house to Jim Newman, a cattleman, for $60.00. Newman bought 1,054 head of cattle and turned them loose on the canyon the following spring. Thus the Yellow House ranch had its beginning in 1882.

About this time the state of Texas set aside 3,050,000 acres of land in northwest Texas to be sold for the purpose of erecting a fine capitol building at Austin, and the Yellow House spring was included in this vast tract that stretched from the Yellow House Canyon north for 200 miles. A group of Chicago people bought 3,000,000 acres of land, and it became the famous XIT ranch. When the Capitol Land Syndicate began to stock the ranch, Newman had to vacate. He moved his cattle to New Mexico in 1886 and established a ranch at a lake about 2 miles east of where Portales now stands. This ranch was also on the Colorado-Ft. Sumner mail route operated by Doak Good and Ben Webb. Good had located at Portales Spring and was running a small herd of cattle there in connection with his mail carrying operations. Good appears to have founded the first ranch on the plains of eastern New Mexico, although he was 14 years behind John S. Chisum, cattle king of the Pecos.

The Capitol Land Syndicate completed the new state house at Austin in 1885; and the Yellow House Canyon became part of the XIT, the greatest cattle ranch in the United States. The Syndicate built some rock houses at Yellow House Spring, and the ranch founded by Jim Newman became the most famous of the seven divisions of the XIT.

Many hardy frontiersmen and wild cowboys worked for the XIT. Billie White was buried on a slope at the foot of the yellow and white cliffs so long ago that no one seems to know how he met his death. Then one of those brave mothers who followed her adventurous husband to the Llano Estacado was laid to rest with her baby in her arms at the Yellow House division of the XIT. A large, unhewn stone with a smaller one nestling at its side tell the tragic tale of the first woman and child to be buried at the Yellow House ranch. Then came Tom Ballard riding wild, high, and handsome only to be killed at Eighteen Mile windmill when this quick-draw man met one who was quicker.

Another to be buried at the Yellow House ranch was a Mexican who froze to death in the great blizzard of 1887. Then came Charlie Ratliff with his jolly cowboy songs and fine saddle. While he was riding night herd on the plains above the canyon the cattle stampeded. In the darkness, Charlie's horse went over the 100 foot cliff, and he was killed. He was laid to rest at the Yellow House ranch with his saddle over his chest in lieu of a coffin. As the years went by rains lowered the earth, and a protruding saddle horn became a gravestone for the cowboy. A rustic poet composed a ballad about poor Charlie. This they sang to restless night herds to quiet them.

The man who did most to make the Yellow House ranch famous was George W. Littlefield. Major Littlefield was born June 23, 1842, in Mississippi, and came to Texas with his parents when 8 years old. At the age of 18 he joined Terry's Texas Rangers. When the Civil War came on, he entered the Confederate army as a second lieutenant. He was made a captain May 1, 1862, and later was promoted to the rank of major. He was badly wounded during the last year of the war and went to Gonzales to recuperate. He took up cattle ranching there when the war ended.

On the broad prairies of South Texas, where the grass was green almost the year round, the Littlefield cattle increased rapidly. When the westward moving railroads crossed the Missouri into Kansas and gave connection with the cattle markets of the East, George W. Littlefield, like many ranchers of his time, began to trail herds to the end of the railroads in Kansas. From these operations he became wealthy.

In his task of creating the Littlefield fortune, he had two able assistants. They were his brother, W. P. Littlefield, and his nephew, J. P. White. When the Comanches were finally driven out of the Staked Plains, Major Littlefield lost no time in sending his nephew to found a ranch on the great plateau. Young Phelps White came up from Gonzales in 1877 with 3,500 head of cows and heifers. Charles Goodnight had already taken possession of Palo Duro Canyon, and White went on to the banks of the South Canadian. A half dozen Mexican families had followed the Canadian down from New Mexico and had founded a little settlement where Atascosa Creek empties into the river from the north. One of the Mexicans had taken possession of a fine spring about 2 miles down the Canadian from the Atascosa settlement.

The spring came to the surface in a pretty valley about a mile from the river and watered several hundred acres of meadow before emptying into the Canadian. Here the grass was stirrup high and green during the driest weather. This was a fine location for a ranch, and James Phelps White gave the Mexican $350.00 to move off and give him possession. Then, where a high cliff gave protection from the cold north winds, he built a house of stone and adobe and erected corrals. Cottonwoods grew along the banks of the Canadian and furnished plenty of fuel and material for the corrals. A ditch from the spring brought water to the house and corrals. This became the LIT ranch, which claimed all on the north side of the river to the New Mexico line as the range of George W. Littlefield. As time went by, a reservoir was constructed to store the water from the spring; and the valley below the house was put under irrigation.

In 1881 Major Littlefield bought John Chisum's Bosque Grande ranch on the Pecos River in New Mexico and sent his brother, W. P. Littlefield, to manage that ranch. Other outfits kept crowding in on the Pecos, however, and the Bosque Grande range became overstocked. The Cass Land and Cattle Company of Pleasant Hill, Missouri, came in 1884 and founded the Bar-V ranch a few miles up the Pecos from Bosque Grande. The chief stockholders were Lee Easley, J. D. Cooley, and W. G. Urton. They bought 2,300 cows and heifers at Ft. Griffin, Texas, and drove them to the Pecos. Easley and Cooley each served a short time as manager of the ranch. Then under the able management of W. G. Urton, the Bar-V became a ranch with approximately 30,000 head of cattle. Urton managed this ranch so successfully that during the nearly 30 years of its existence not a cowboy was killed on the ranch by horse or man. When the ranch was closed out, there were 5,000 head more Bar-V cattle on the range than the books of the company had indicated.

With the range along the Pecos overstocked, drought struck in 1885. The Pecos stopped running above Salt Creek. Cattle gathered around the water holes and died by the hundred. Major Littlefield and has associates then bought another ranch on the Staked Plains of New Mexico east of Roswell. This was the Four Lakes ranch. There was little water on the Plains, and the Littlefields had the whole country to themselves. They drilled wells and erected windmills; and, while other ranchers went broke, Major Littlefield and his brother and nephew continued to prosper.

They soon acquired another ranch on the Plains. A Mexican, choosing the rainy season when the fresh-water lakes had water in them, went into the unexplored region east of Bosque Grande. About 40 miles south west of Portales Spring he found a great mesa rising high above the treeless, waterless plain. Knowing that he could find springs only in broken country, the Mexican began to search the canyons around the mesa near where Elida and Kenna now stand. In a draw almost in the center of the mesa he found the grass unusually green. No one but a pioneer would have noticed the difference in the vegetation, but the green grass told the Mexican that water was near the surface of the ground. He stuck his shovel into the earth, and it struck something hard. He pryed it up and found it to be a cedar pole. Clods tumbled into the opening where the pole had been and splashed into water. Investigation revealed a spring. Indians had found it long ago and had walled it up with rock. Then in order to keep the white men from finding the water, they had covered the spring with poles and spread sand over it. In time the spring was overgrown with grass. Then the rising moisture that kept the grass green revealed the spring to the Mexican. The Littlefields gave the native $700.00 for his spring, and it became another ranch that was not crowded for many years. W. P. Littlefield took charge of this Hidden Spring ranch, while White managed the Four Lakes ranch.

Major Littlefield also bought an irrigated tract 4 miles east of Roswell, New Mexico. This fertile spot was watered by artesian wells. Here he raised fine bulls and rams to improve the Littlefield herds. The LFD, as this ranch was known, became one of the show places of the Pecos Valley. Here were several hundred acres of alfalfa and a commercial apple orchard. Peacocks strutted on the Bermuda lawns, black tailed deer grazed in the park before the foreman's house, and a huge black bear staked out on the lawn paced to and fro until he outgrew his collar and the cowboys choked him to death with their lariats while trying to change it.

In 1900 Major Littlefield and associates bought the Yellow House division of the XIT ranch. The price paid for the 275,000 acre tract was $2.00 per acre. A group of good ranch buildings were erected at the spring on Yellow House canyon, and this became the headquarters of the ranch. The buildings consisted of a bunk house for the cowboys; a kitchen and dining room; a house for the foreman, J. W. Roberts; and a house for the owner of the ranch. All were painted in the traditional yellow.

The spring had been gradually drying up, so a well was drilled to take its place. A windmill was placed over this. In order to get the fans of the mill up above surrounding cliffs, what was said to be the highest windmill tower in the world was erected. This mill was 128 feet above the ground. It was so high that none of the cowboys wanted to grease it. The foreman made the men take turns at this hazardous task, and many a green hand found it convenient to quit just before it came his turn to ascend the tower that swayed amid the whirlwinds of the Staked Plains.

Although the Yellow House ranch was fenced and crossed fenced, it required 15 cowboys to look after the 25,000 head of cattle on the ranch. From 5,000 to 6,000 calves were branded each season. During the first ten years the Littlefields owned the property, it produced over $1,000,-000 worth of cattle. All the land except a small strip along the canyon was as level as a floor. In time it became too valuable for grazing purposes, and the ranch was cut up into small tracts and put on the market as farm lands. The first unit was offered for sale in 1912 at from $25.00 to $35.00 per acre on easy terms at 6 per cent interest. It sold rapidly. Figured at $25.00 per acre, the Littlefields had made over 100 per cent on their money every year for twelve years, to say nothing of the cattle it had produced. This ranch that had cost Major Littlefield and his associates a little over a half million dollars had become worth $6,875,000 at the lowest estimate.

A town was laid out and named Littlefield after the great cattleman. The town grew into a small city, and the Yellow House ranch soon became Lamb County, one of the banner cotton counties of Texas. By 1923 all except the rough region along the canyon was in cultivation.

At the height of his career Major Littlefield owned approximately 50,000 head of cattle. The chief brands used were LIT and LFD.

Not content with his extensive cattle business, Major Littlefield went to Austin in 1883 and with a capital of less than $100,000 established the American National Bank of Austin. This institution specialized in cattle loans, and no one knew better than George W. Littlefield what it took to make a good cattle loan. He had a personal acquaintance with every cattleman of importance in the Southwest. He knew their integrity, their business ability, and he knew cattle security. With the help of men like J. P. White, Whitfield Harral, and H. A. Wroe, he built a bank with resources of $10,000,000. While other Texas banks struggled with a deluge of little cotton loans, the American National Bank of Austin was getting most of the big, easily handled cattle loans. Other banks did a cattle loan business, too; but they could hardly compete with a man like Major Littlefield, who knew the cow business from A to Z.

A beautiful 9-story bank and office building was erected at the corner of Sixth and Congress Avenue in Austin. This fireproof building is of brick trimmed with grey Texas granite. The main corridor is Pavonazzi marble. The massive doors are of solid bronze. The door handles are copper steer heads. Inside the building are mural paintings of scenes on the Yellow House Ranch west of Lubbock and the lovely irrigated farm at Roswell, New Mexico. A great eagle, killed on The Yellow House Canyon, was mounted and stood with wings spread at the main entrance.

By 1920, when the great cattleman died at Austin, most of the Yellow House Ranch was in cultivation. What remained became the property of his nephew, J. P. White, as did the Four Lakes and LFD ranches. Major Littlefield's brother, W. P. Littlefield, became the owner of the Hidden Spring Ranch at Kenna, New Mexico, that he had managed for so many years. When W. P. Littlefield died in 1927, this ranch was divided between his son, G. T. Littlefield, and his nephew, Pat Boone.

James Phelps White proved to be almost as good a cattleman and money maker as his famous uncle. When Major Littlefield established his first ranch in the Panhandle of Texas, it was 21 year old Phelps White who drove the herd from Gonzales to the Canadian. When the famous cattleman bought Chisum's ranch at Bosque Grande on the Pecos in New Mexico, White drove three big herds across the almost waterless Llano Estacado to the Pecos. Young White became manager of the ranch at Four Lakes and gradually acquired a larger interest in the far flung ranching operations of his uncle. He became part owner in the Yellow House ranch when Major Littlefield bought that property.

After the death of his uncle, Phelps White acquired the remainder of the Yellow House ranch, the LFD east of Roswell, Bosque Grande, and the Four Lakes ranch. In 1929 he bought the 120,000 acre Long Arroyo ranch from the Hagerman estate. This ranch is in Chavez County, about 20 miles east of Roswell, New Mexico.

Major Littlefield and Phelps White both gave large sums to philantropic causes. Mr. Littlefield's bequests totaled $3,000,000. Most of this went to the University of Texas. The Wrenn Library was his personal gift to that institution. His palatial residence was left to the school for a home for the president and became the property of that institution upon the death of Mrs. Littlefield, January 10, 1935.

J. P. White probably did more charitable work than any man in Roswell, New Mexico, his home town. He frequently sent food and clothing to needy families and gave positive instructions to delivery wagons of the stores not to tell who sent the things.

James Phelps White made his last trip across the Staked Plains in the fall of 1934. This time it was an airplane instead of a broncho that furnished the transportation, and the rancher was seeking the aid of skilled physicians instead of new pastures for lowing herds. Down the trail into the land from which he had come 50 years earlier went the cattleman to die. Death came at San Antonio, October 21, 1934. The body was returned to Roswell for burial, and every store in town closed during the funeral out of respect to another great cowboy who had gone to the last roundup.

Before his death, J. P. White gave the remainder of the Yellow House ranch to his son, George White. A modern brick house in the traditional yellow was erected to take the place of the old ranch house that burned. There on 23,000 acres with 1,000 high grade Herefords the young man continued in the occupation of his ancestors. Visitors at the ranch may still see the tumbled down fort on the cliff above the spring and the old bunkhouse where cowboys unrolled their beds when blizzards drove them from beneath the stars.

Chapter VIII.

ISAAC L. ELWOOD AND THE SPADE

The Ranch That Thorn Wire Built

America has had many illustrious cattle kings, but Isaac L. Elwood, barron of the Spade ranches, made them all pay tribute, be they large or small. This man who made debtors of the other cattlemen was the inventor of the "thorn wire" fence, which made possible the fencing of the Western range.

Isaac L. Elwood was a farmer living in the vicinity of De Kalb, Illinois, when he made the discovery that brought a stream of royalty from all who lived in the plains. Smooth wire had already come into use, but cattle paid little attention to it. They did show some respect for thorn hedges, however; and Ellwood began to ask himself: "why not make a thorny wire?" While attending a fair at De Kalb about 1873 he saw some fence made by hanging thin pieces of wood on wire, the wood containing spikes which stock kept away from. He went home determined to make wire with thorns on it. The first barbwire was a ribbon of iron with spikes on its edges. The projections were turned in all directions by twisting the ribbon. This flat wire was too heavy and expensive to be very satisfactory, and Ellwood went to work on the idea of fastening thorns on round smooth wire. In time, he found that by curling the barbs around a smooth wire, they could be held in place and evenly spaced by twisting the barbed wire with another slick wire. He patented his idea, and paved the way for settlement of the great prairies where there was no timber for rail fences.

When Ellwood started manufacturing barbwire, he cut and twisted his barbs in an old coffee grinder. A boy was put up on a windmill tower to string the barbs on a round, smooth wire. A grindstone was used to twist this wire with another smooth strand to hold the barbs in place. A man standing at the grindstone spaced the barbs as the two strands came together.

This wire sold at 2 cents a pound, but even then it was lots cheaper than split rails. It proved to be immensely popular on the prairies where there was neither stone or timber for fencing purposes. A few farmers had tried to enclose their land with thorn hedges; but "thorn wire" had this outclassed, too. Miles of barbwire could be put up in a few days while it took years to grow a thorn hedge fence. Also barbwire did not sap the ground or take up valuable space like a hedge.

The demand for wire exceeded the supply of Ellwood's makeshift factory. J. F. Glidden, a neighboring farmer, became Ellwood's partner; and an improved factory was erected at De Kalb. They bought other patents and bought out other wire manufacturing concerns until they had a monopoly. Ellwood also invented several types of woven wire. The consolidated concerns eventually became the American Fence Co., with Isaac L. Ellwood drawing royalty on every pound of wire sold.

When the wire company began to sell in Texas, a big demonstration was held at San Antonio. Wild longhorns were driven into a corral composed of eight or ten wires and told to do their worst. The hides of the cattle were thick and tough, but a few runs on the heavily spiked wire were enough. The fence held the animals without seriously injuring them, and the farmers and ranchers were convinced.

Farmers on the prairies could now keep stock off their crops, and the hatred that the Kansas and Oklahoma homesteaders had for the stockman began to subside. Ranchers found that their cattle could be held on their home range without the expense of line riders. They could also improve their herds by segregating their stock from the scrub males of their neighbors.

Texas farmers and stockmen took to the barbwire idea quickly, and the Lone Star state became one of Ellwood's best markets. While promoting the sale of his wire in that state, he met the Snyder Brothers, owners of two big ranches, one on the Staked Plains and the other at the foot of the Plains.

During the early 70's Captain Renderbrook, United States army officer, was killed by Indians at a spring in what is now Mitchell County. The watering place where he fell became the headquarters of J. Taylor Barr, who started ranching there before the country was entirely free of Indians. The first ranch house was a 2-room structure made of chittum poles with a thatched roof and dirt floor. On one side was a shed-room made by stretching buffalo hides over a framework of poles. Barr's brand was BO.

D. H. and J. W. Snyder bought this ranch in 1882 and changed the brand to JF. A lumber bunkhouse was erected to take the place of the pole structure. The cattle that the Snyder brothers bought for stocking the ranch were from the herds of Andy Long of Sweetwater.

Soon after the Snyders came into possession of the Renderbrook Spring, the Texas Pacific railroad built through the country and a large part of their range was deeded to the railway company as a bonus for constructing the new line. The Snyder Brothers began to buy and lease railroad lands and had a ranch of 130,000 acres when Ellwood began to negotiate with them for the property. The Snyders had begun improving their stock by importing Shorthorn bulls. John Frank Yearwood was foreman of the Renderbrook ranch and had played an important part in putting the property on a paying basis.

Ellwood acquired the Renderbrook ranch and began his career as a Texas cattle king in 1889. He stocked the ranch with cattle he bought from J. F. Evans, who had a ranch on Saddler creek 10 miles northeast of Clarendon. The cattle were paid for with barbwire. This stock bore the Spade (☐—1) brand, which had been recorded in Donley County July 11, 1883. The Spade cattle were moved to the Renderbrook ranch; and from that date on, all Ellwood stock bore the Spade brand, which became known from Texas to Montana.

Believing that the broad prairie of the Staked Plains with its miles and miles of gamma and mesquite grass was even better than the Renderbrook range, the Snyders had bought 128,000 acres 25 miles northwest of where Lubbock now stands. It was as level as a floor and was one of the finest tracts of grass in the world. Cattle suffered less from heat on the high, cool plain. The dry atmosphere with its constant wind kept down harassing insects, and the Snyder cattle flourished there. The only drawback was the blizzards that occasionally swept over the great open world. In order to prevent their cattle from drifting during the storms, the Snyder Brothers enclosed this ranch with a 6-wire fence. Building of the great fences, plus too rapid expansion, got the Snyders into financial difficulties. They sold the land to Mr. Ellwood and moved their JF cattle to Coldwater Creek in Sherman County, 125 miles north of Amarillo.

Although cattle on both the Ellwood ranches were branded Spade, the ranch northwest of Lubbock was called the "Spade Ranch" while that in Mitchell County continued to be known as the "Renderbrook Ranch". Supplies for the ranch on the Staked Plains were hauled from Colorado,

Texas, a distance of 150 miles. Snyder Brothers obtained supplies for their Sherman County ranch from Liberal, Kan.

Isaac Ellwood's barbwire business kept him in the North most of the time; so he appointed his son, W. L. Ellwood, manager of the Spade ranches. This vast open country with its antelope, wild horses, and slick cattle fascinated the young man from Illinois; and he soon became a full fledged cattleman. He never ceased to love the lowing herds and the carefree life of the range. He made many trips to the East, but he was never happy until back on the Spade with a good horse between his knees.

To W. L. Ellwood fell the task of stocking and improving the Spade ranches. Although all material had to be hauled long distances, only the best improvements were placed on the property. The headquarters ranch northwest of Lubbock was piped for water; and the men who had never used anything but a canteen and water keg were supplied with hot and cold water and bath. A carbide lighting system was installed to take the place of smokey lanterns in general use.

Huge dipping vats were constructed to rid the cattle of ticks and other infections common in the lower altitudes of Texas. Numerous cross-fences reduced the labor of the cowboys, and glittering windmills poured their crystal streams into round stave tanks in the heart of the pastures.

W. L. Ellwood made his home at the Lubbock division and, under the advice of his father, bought land until the Spade ranch consisted of 272,000 acres. It was 8 to 12 miles wide and 54 miles long. The last big purchase was in 1906 when 12 leagues were acquired from the Lake-Tomb Cattle Co. and added to the Spade ranch.

The Arnett Brothers, Tom and Bass, took over the management of the Spade ranch for W. L. Ellwood in 1906.

Among the many picturesque characters who worked for the Spade outfit was J. Frank Norfleet. This cowboy and range boss gradually accumulated a small fortune only to be swindled out of his life's savings, $35,000, by a ring of confidence men. Full of the fighting spirit typical of men who ride the range, Norfleet turned amateur detective and went after the gang that is said to have made a million dollars from their unlawful plots. Of him it was said: "He ran down and threw together the biggest herd of bunco swindlers ever put into one pen at a single instance."

In speaking to his son, Isaac L. Ellwood often said: "I may not live to see it, but the time will come when the Staked Plains will be almost entirely in cultivation, and the land our cattle graze will be worth $40 to $50 an acre." He died in 1910 and did not live to see the great cow ranches turned into farms.

W. L. Ellwood loved the life of the range and hated to see the Spade ranch broken up. Settlers who bought the land in Texas and homesteaders in New Mexico's part of the Staked Plains proved that the great prairie was a good farming country, especially the eastern portion. The Spade lands became too valuable for grazing purposes; and the North Spade pasture of 90,000 acres was placed on the market in 1925. At the end of the first year, 80 per cent of this tract had been sold for farming purposes. About 170,000 acres of the 272,000 acre ranch had been sold by 1937. Most of the tracts are of 160 or 320 acres. When the depression of the '30s came on and the farmers who had bought the land on easy terms were having difficulty in meeting their payment, Mr. Ellwood bought their cotton at 2 cents a pound or more above the market price. Most of the farmers came from Oklahoma and East Texas. The rich prairie soil is not poisoned up with weeds or parasites, and the level nature of the land makes it well adapted to the use of tractors and improved farm machinery. In 1931 Lamb county, where much of the Spade land is located, ranked first in lint cotton production in Texas, averaging 287 pounds of lint to the acre. Kaffir and Maize are grown for hogs and poultry. Numerous dairy herds have taken the place of the Herefords on that part of the ranch that has been sold to farmers.

Although more than half of the North Spade had been sold when World War II came on, some cattle were still being raised on the ranch.

The Renderbrook ranch was still flourishing. No part of it had been sold. In fact, 32,000 acres had been added. Although part of that ranch was devoted to sheep raising, there were still about 15,000 head of cattle on the Spade ranches. The sheep pastures had been fenced with wolf proof wire, invented by Isaac L. Ellwood and manufactured in plants owned by the Ellwoods.

W. L. Ellwood was manager of the Spade ranches until his death in 1933. His brother, E. P. Ellwood, and W. F. Eisenberger, were appointed executors of the estate. Tom Arnett was foreman of the North Spade and Otto Jones was in charge at the Renderbrook ranch.

E. P. Ellwood built a beautiful winter home called the "White House", on the Renderbrook ranch. This modern house stood on a slight elevation that gave an excellent view of the ranch. A short distance from the "White House" was the home of the ranch foreman and the bunkhouse of the cowboys, all of stone. All the buildings were piped for gas that came from two wells on the ranch. This headquarters was not far from the spring where Capt. Renderbrook lost his life fighting Indians.

Although the Renderbrook division of the Spade outfit is up-to-date, it is still a real cow ranch in every sense of the word. At sunrise you will find the foreman at the corrals giving instructions as the cowboys catch their horses and break for the hills.

When roundup time comes, out comes the chuck wagon with its rolls of bedding and pots and pans. The cook climbs to his seat and cracks his whip over a good team. The wagon boss tells the cook and horse wrangler where to have the wagon and remuda at noon. The cowboys are led to a point where they fan out and begin to comb the hills and ravines. Toward noon they converge where the cook is waiting with beefsteak and "sour dough". The tired punchers dismount and wash as the cook yells, "Chow. Come and get it or I'll throw it out!" This was the practice back in the days when ranching was at its height, and it is still the practice on the Renderbrook division of the Spade.

CHAPTER IX.

CAMPBELL AND MACKENZIE OF THE MATADORS
A $19,000,000 Ranch.

The Matador Land & Cattle Co., Ltd., operating two big ranches on the rim of the Staked Plains, is one of the greatest American cattle concerns of all time. It held the largest acreage on the Staked Plains in 1951, and is probably the largest in the United States if figured on a cattle population basis. Its only rival for first place in the nation is the King Ranch in Southwest Texas.

This great ranch was running 47,000 head of cattle on 800,000 acres of land in 1951. It was founded in 1878 by Henry Harrison Campbell, a Texan. Campbell was a sandy haired man with a birthmark that covered half his face. On the range he was known as "Paint" Campbell because of the birthmark.

Campbell began his career as an ordinary cowboy during the period of expansion that followed the Civil War. By 1876 he had saved enough to buy a small herd, which he drove to California and sold at a good profit. With the money he made on this trail trip, he founded the Matador Ranch near the rim of the Caprock on the eastern edge of the Staked Plains, where hunters were rapidly exterminating the buffalo for their hides. It is said that seven million buffalo were killed on the Western Plains, leaving behind a vast empire for cattlemen.

Campbell followed the MacKenzie trail up to the Caprock, the eastern rim of the great plateau of the Staked Plains, and bought out a squatter by the name of Joe Brown, who had taken possession of Ballard Spring near the head of the

Pease River. The spring had received its name from a hunter named Ballard. Brown had a few hogs but had not tried to run cattle with the buffalo.

The spring was in the rough country under the rim of the Caprock where the cattle could go out on the vast prairie of the Staked Plains in summer and retire to the timber breaks for winter shelter. The Plains were treeless, but the breaks contained considerable mesquite, cedar, and hackberry. There were also large strips covered with "shinoak". It was the acorns of the shinnery that supported Joe Brown's hogs.

H. H. "Paint" Campbell was quick to see the opportunity for a vast cattle kingdom in this region that had supported millions of buffalo. He returned to Ft. Worth and in 1879 organized the Matador Cattle Co. with a capital of $50,000. Matador is a Spanish word meaning "bull fighter".

Campbell stocked his range with 8,000 Jingle Bob cows and heifers from John Chisum's outfit on the Pecos in New Mexico. The cattle were purchased from Robert K. Wiley and Thomas Coggins, who had been business associates of the great cattleman and who had taken the stock on a mortgage, or in payment of a note.

The first Matador Ranch headquarters was a half-dugout in a hillside. When Elizabeth Bundy Campbell, wife of H. H. Campbell, arrived at the Matador ranch, she insisted on having something a little more civilized to live in; and a small box house was constructed. The lumber for this building was secured from a sawmill at Ft. Griffin, 150 miles to the southeast.

When this cowgirl arrived in West Texas, there were only three white women in the entire area. They were Mrs. Cooper, wife of an Indian trader at Tepee City, 20 miles away; Mrs. Hank Smith on Blanco Canyon, 45 miles away; and Mrs. Charles Goodnight at Palo Duro Canyon, 60 miles north. Tepee City, once a great camp ground for the Indians, was now more of a trading post for buffalo hunters. Ranching on the plains was a lonely life, and Mrs. Campbell traded a sack of flour for a black dog to keep her company while her hsuband rode the range.

Campbell's cattle multiplied rapidly on the unlimited range, the calf crop averaging from 75 to 80 per cent each year. Destruction by lobo wolves and death from old age were practically the only losses. Heifer calves became cows in 2 years and added their production to that of the original herd. The Matador Cattle Co. began to buy and lease land from the state. The land was sold on easy terms, some of it on 40 year time; consequently it did not take much capital to control a lot of acreage. By 1884 Campbell was working 20 men and had 1,000,000 acres in his ranch, most of which was leased land. In 1885, just six years after he organized the Matador Cattle Co., Campbell and his associates sold to a Scotch syndicate for $1,250,000; and the name of the company was changed to the Matador Land & Cattle Co., Ltd. Under the terms of the sale, H. H. Campbell remained with the company as superintendent of the Matador ranch. W. F. Summerville became general manager of the big organization. Home offices were in Dundee, Scotland. General offices were maintained in Ft. Worth. A well stocked commissary at the ranch supplied the cowboys with clothing, bedding, tobacco, ammunition, and other articles not furnished at the expense of the company. This merchandise was forwarded by freight wagons from Ft. Worth.

In the days before the introduction of barbwire fences, few cattlemen knew exactly how much stock they had. Since it was the custom to hold the steers until they were fully grown or 4 years old, ranchers usually estimated the number of cattle at the calf crop, plus four times its number. The

Matadors branded 10,525 calves in 1888 and must have had about 50,000 head of cattle. Although the cowboys tried to hold the stock on the home range, the Matador cattle were scattered more or less all over the Staked Plains. In 1888 Mat Pierce brought back 204 head from New Mexico. Campbell reported having 203 bulls after selling 115. Even at this early period, 500 acres was planted in oats for wintering the saddle horses; and some attempt was made to feed poor cows.

The Ft. Worth & Denver railway built through the country 60 miles to the northeast, and all supplies for the Matador ranch were hauled from Childress after that date. A buckboard stage connected the ranch with Childress, the nearest railway point. Before the building of this line, most of the Matador cattle were sold on the range or were driven to Dodge City, Kansas. Campbell sold at all ages, depending on the demand. He experimented with feeding and came to the conclusion that the most money could be made on young animals.

The company was paying 4 cents an acre for the land it had under lease. Crosby County valued the Matador horses at $30 each for taxation. Two year old steers brought from $14.00 to $16.00 per head on the range.

Cattle belonging to other ranchers sometimes became mixed with herds on the trail. If these were not discovered and cut out before the herd got off the range of the owner, they were taken on to market and sold. The honest trail-drivers forwarded the proceeds to the owner of the stock. Not all stockmen were scrupulous and prompt in this matter, however; and prosecution and killings sometimes resulted. There seems to have been no complaint against Mr. Campbell in his long record of ranching in West Texas. In fact there are many letters in the files of the company like the one he wrote to the Espuela Land & Cattle Co., one of his neighbors to the south, notifying them that he had 30 head of Spur cattle and had branded 5 calves for them.

There were 69 men on the Matador payroll through the summer of 1889, with a monthly payroll of $1,989.25. The spring roundup began on June 5 that year. Two or three weeks before starting the work, Campbell wrote all the surrounding ranchers inviting them to send representatives to look after any of their stock that might be mixed with the Matador cattle.

One of the wagons started on the head of Tepee Creek and worked down. The other began at Williams Dugout on Croton. The roundup lasted 40 days. Eight horses was the minimum for each cowboy. These were ridden on the grass, and men changed mounts two or three times a day. Roping and cutting horses were reserved for their special work. Night horses were saddled and staked where they would be ready for the owner to mount when roused for his period of night guard. Night-herding was divided into three periods, with two men on duty at a time riding in opposite directions around the herd.

Night herding, during the roundup or on the trail, was often full of adventure. Soon after dark the first animals, with grunts like they were deflating themselves, would sink to the ground to doze and chew their cuds. Others would follow their example, and soon the whole herd would be resting. About midnight, cattle get up to stretch and to relieve themselves. If the range is good and they are not hungry, they will return to their rest and remain until morning, provided a lobo wolf or a hail storm does not stampede them. Hail is the worst thing that can strike a herd, but a skunk is often all that is necessary for a wild stampede. Only a man who has followed cattle by the flash of lightning and had his clothes torn off by mesquite and chaparral can fully understand what a stampede means. Big steers can run 15 or 20 miles, and it is almost impossible to hold them when they start. Circle the leaders and keep up the drags was a general policy during a stampede. It was the mesquite thorns, cat-claw, and tree cactus in such occasions that led to the development of leather chaps.

There were usually 25 men with each wagon during the Matador roundups. With 10 or 12 horses for each cowboy, the remuda contained 250 to 300 animals. M. Cammack, New Mexico lawyer and rancher, is one of the many who once wrangled horses for the Matadors. The ranch raised its own horses, using Morgan and Steeldust stallions with the range mares.

With the cowboys spread out fan shaped, the Matadors drove down the creeks. When the herds became too large to handle efficiently, a halt was made for the branding. Two ropers, or snakers, dragged the calves from the herds. Large calves were roped by the heels; small ones by the neck. The flankers worked in pairs. Taking turns about, these men would rush up on the left side of the animals, reach over their backs and get a hold in the flank, lift up, and bring the animal down on their sides. When the calf hit the ground, one man seized its head and kept it from getting its fore feet under it while the other placed one foot against the lower hock and stretched the upper hind leg back and held it while a third man applied the smoking iron and a fourth marked the ears. This method is commonly used today.

The Matador brand is a V that looks much like 7-V. It has been called a "Flying V", but it is not. The location of the brand has been changed from time to time but most often was on the left side and thigh. A tally brand on the shoulder indicated the age of the animal; for example, in 1907 it was a 7. The horses are branded 50 on the left hip. Most horses, like men, are right handed. This makes them work best on the left side of a cow. For this reason, many ranchers perfer to have their brands on the left side. The Matador ear mark is a crop of the right ear. The number of calves branded is determined by counting the ear markings.

The best calf crop that H. H. Campbell ever claimed was 92 per cent. He set 25,000 as his goal for a calf crop but never quite reached that number.

By 1890 the Matador Land & Cattle Co., Ltd., owned 140,000 acres of land in fee simple and had paid out $150,-000 to the state and to individuals for leases. In that year Campbell wrote the home office that Texas was on the eve of a land boom. As he predicted a period of more active land buying began soon after.

W. F. Summerville, general manager of the Matador Land & Cattle Co., Ltd., resigned in 1891 and was succeeded by Murdo MacKenzie. There was some dissatisfaction with Campbell's management of the Matador ranch, and the home office asked for his resignation in 1891. This was a heavy blow to the man who had built up one of the largest ranches in America, but Campbell bore his loss with fortitude. He met MacKenzie at the end of '91 and conducted him over the ranch. In his farewell address, he urged his cowboys to make themselves useful and law-abiding citizens in the country they had pioneered. He advised them to take advantage of the liberal land laws, acquire property and thus provide for their future.

Campbell had only a few sections of land when he lost his job. From being a cattle king with unlimited European capital behind him, he suddenly found himself a stock-farmer in the dry region of the Staked Plains. He went to the town of Matador, 3 miles north of the Headquarters of the Matador ranch, and became County Judge of the newly organized Motley County. Mrs. Campbell became Postmistress. The town, however, was almost surrounded by the great Matador ranch. Its growth was slow and the Campbells had to struggle. When this great cow man died in 1911, however, he left his son, Harry Campbell, in fairly prosperous circumstances. This young man, the first white child born in Motley County, lives at his ranch 10 miles west of Matador.

After 1891 the Matador outfit became the biography of Murdo MacKenzie, who came out from the Old Country full of Scotch thrift and executive ability. Under his management, the Matadors spread northward into Canada and southward into Brazil. A. J. Ligertwood became superintendent of the ranch on the edge of the Staked Plains.

Before the building of the Ft. Worth and Denver, the Matadors marketed many of their cattle at Dodge City, Kansas, but they drove their last herd to Dodge in 1893. After that date, most of the steers were trailed to the Far North and finished their growth on ranches in Montana and the Dakotas. John Smith was the most famous of the trail bosses. He spent 16 summers on the trail with Matador cattle.

In 1904 the Matador Land & Cattle Co., Ltd., bought the Alamocita division of the XIT. This tract northwest of Amarillo contained over 400,000 acres. The same year they leased 500,000 acres in the Cheyenne reservation in South Dakota. D. Summerville became manager of the South Dakota ranch. Con McMurray was wagon boss. Walker Crump was the youngest man in the group of Texas cowboys that went to the northern state to work for the Matadors. The cattle that were sent to this ranch were shipped from Channing. They were unloaded at Everts, S D., and crossed the Missouri River on a pontoon bridge. Although the climate was severe and only steers could stand it, the Matador cattle grew large and strong and put on heavy coats of fat in preparation for the long winters. When they were fully grown, they went to the Omaha and Chicago markets.

There were 700 saddle horses on the Matador ranch in South Dakota. More than once the remuda had to be used to break trail for the cattle when heavy snows fell. Although valleys were often impassable in winter, the Chinook winds usually cleared the hillsides sufficiently for stock to graze. Poor animals perished, but steers that went into the winter fat came through, unless they fell victim to wolves or died from having their feet cut and frozen by ice. The Missouri some times froze over in winter, and there were times when both wagons and cattle crossed on the ice. A winter or two of this was usually sufficient for the Texas cowboys. Crump stayed in South Dakota five years, however, before returning to the Staked Plains.

The Matadors also leased 500,000 acres on the Saskatchewan River in Canada. The first shipment to this ranch numbered 2,200 2-year olds and was unloaded at Waldeen, Canada.

In 1913 the Matador Land & Cattle Co., Ltd., leased 550,000 acres of the Ft. Belknap Indian Reservation, near Bear Paw and Harlem, Montana. A year or two later they bought Walt Coburn's Circle-C ranch of 20,000 acres adjoining their Ft. Belknap lease. They also acquired the DeRicquies ranch 85 miles east of the Coburn property. Coburn was a well known cowboy author.

Each ranch had its own superintendent. Murdo MecKenzie, general manager, spent most of his time making the rounds from one property to another in general supervision of the far flung enterprises. William McKay, president of the Matador Land & Cattle Co., Ltd., came to America once each year for an inspection of the ranch on the Staked Plains, the chief breeding ground for the Matador cattle. The only time he missed was during the submarine campaign of World War I.

MacKenzie also went to South America to look after the ranch property that owners of the Matadors acquired in Brazil. A few American cowboys went down to South America with MacKenzie to work under a 2-year contract. John Jackson was one of these. Jackson, upon his return, said the ranch in Brazil was in a region infested with jaguars and boa constrictors. It looked like a swamp to the Texas cowboy, who had been used to the high, dry atmosphere of the Staked Plains. Horses did not do well in the heat, and sometimes the cowboys had to ride mules. These animals seldom were good at roping or cutting cattle.

One day the boys from Texas heard their dog barking at something in a swamp. Jackson jumped on his mule and loped down to see what the dog was after. Before he arrived, the dog suddenly began to yelp with distress. His cries ceased as suddenly as they had began. When the cowboy arrived he found that a huge boa constrictor had crushed the dog and was swallowing him head first.

Lobo wolves were an ever present menace to the Matador herds of the Staked Plains. The huge wolves usually brought down their victims by cutting their ham strings. When the tendons had been cut, and the animal could neither run nor fight, the killers sometimes made a meal off the helpless beast while it was still alive. They ate calves and colts mostly, but a pair could kill a fully grown steer when necessary.

The Matadors imported hounds from England to hunt these wolves that often were too cunning to be trapped or poisoned with success. Several breeds of dogs were tried. Staghounds and greyhounds that ran by sight were fast and good for coyotes, but they were of little use on the lobos that usually worked at night and remained concealed during the daytime. The long ears of the American black and tan hounds got in the way when fighting the grey killers. Black and white fox hounds appeared to be the best for both trailing and fighting. Two men gave their full time to hunting the lobos, and many other cowboys participated for the sport it gave. Dock Backster hunted with a pack of hounds in the Croton breaks. Buck Curry hunted from Turtle Hole camp. Later, Claude Jeffers mixed some hunting with his bronc breaking.

No one ever went after lobos with less than 20 dogs. If they did, the wolves turned and cleaned up on the hounds. One snap from the powerful jaws of a lobo was sufficient to ruin a dog for life.

The hounds usually caught and killed a coyote in 15 or 20 minutes after they struck a fresh trail. Lobos were something different. Jeffers says that these wolves could run as fast as the best horses and could run all day. The lobos would either eat the pack up or hit it out in a straight run for 15 or 20 miles. They did not change their course for hills, cliffs, or ravines. In fact, the rougher the country the better it suited these great stock killers. Sometimes they took the hounds clear out of the country, and the dogs would be days getting back to the ranch.

The hunters, mounted on good horses, followed the dogs as closely as possible and shot the wolves when they were bayed. A big pack of the black and white hounds could kill a lobo, but the loss in ruined and wounded dogs was always large. In reporting the work of the hunters, Campbell said Backster and Curry killed 7 in three days in 1891.

Any one who killed a lobo could get $5.00 for the scalp by presenting it at the Matador ranch. As high as 500 coyotes were killed in a single year by the Matador hunters. The big wolves were pretty well thinned out by 1900, although Claude Jeffers killed a big fellow after 1910. The lobo had just finished a heavy meal and could not run. He backed up against a cliff and kept the dogs off until the cowboy shot him.

Jeffers once got three bobcats and five coyotes out of one den.

"Business surely picked up when the dogs followed a coyote into that nest of varments. There were almost as many cats and coyotes as hounds, and several dogs came out of the cave with bobcats sitting on their backs. One dog got hung in the den and spent several days shrinking up until he got small enough to get loose. He came home with his ribs showing and half starved.

"When traveling, the hounds would often string out and go through the same movements like a company of soldiers. I once passed a big rattlesnake and looked back to see what the dogs would do. The lead hound heard the rattler and jumped to one side as he came even with the snake. The others executed the same movement, and all passed unharmed," Jeffers said.

An amusing story has been told about Turtle Hole camp. Among the men who came over from the Old Country to work for the Matadors was an Englishman who had a conceited opinion of the greatness and superiority of his own country. The Matador ponies were good, but the horses were bigger and better in England. England had bigger and better cattle, too. After listening to an endless number of things that were bigger and better in England, the Texas cowboys got tired of it. One night when the outfit was camped at Turtle Hole, one of the boys caught a hard-shell turtle and put him in the Englishman's bed. When the fellow discovered something in his blankets, he sprang out of bed. Seeing the thing wiggle the cover he began to shout; "What is it? What is it?"

"It is just a bed bug. Why all the excitement? Surely you must have them bigger and better in England," they told him.

Another "green-horn" from England came into one of the line camps, where he had been assigned to work, complaining that he had nearly starved to death for water on his way out from the Matador Headquarters.

"How is that?" they asked him. "The trail passed a windmill and crossed a creek?"

"I didn't have a cup," was the astonishing reply.

Even today the Matador cowboys will tell you stories of the thrift of the Scotch owners of the ranch. It is said that on one of his trips to the ranch, McKay asked the manager how many calves the Matadors would get that year. "About 10,000", he replied. When the manager made his report to the home office in Dundee, it was just 27 under his estimate of the calf crop; and the foreman was congratulating himself on this indication of almost superhuman knowledge of cattle. When McKay wrote back, he wanted to know where the other 27 calves were.

The 420,000 acres at Matador, Texas, on the eastern edge of the Staked Plains has always been the most valuable of the Matador holdings. Most of the land was acquired from the railways that had received the land as a bonus for constructing new lines. When Texas passed the 4-section law, many of the Matador cowboys filed on land and sold it to the Matadors when they had acquired title to it.

Next in importance was the Alamocita division northwest of Amarillo. The Montana and Dakota ranches were gradually reduced or converted to sheep raising. The company had no cattle in Canada in 1951, the year the Matador holdings sold for $19,000,000.

At this time, there were 14 line camps on the big ran at Matador, Texas. From one to a half dozen cowboys were stationed at each camp throughout the year. The McDonald camp may be taken as typical of the stations from which the cowboys work. At the time the author first visited the

Matadors, McDonald camp was a 3-room house in a ravine where a windmill poured its crystal stream into a large, round tank with its string of water troughs. There was a bunk room, a kitchen, and a living room. The cowboys had converted the living room into a small museum of ranch life. On the walls were the horns of longhorn steers, deer antlers, and the head of a buffalo. There were cruel Spanish bridle bits, old spurs, historic guns, old branding irons. There was a model chuck wagon with its chuck box, wagon bows, and water kegs. There was, also, an example of the famous trigger gate corral used in the trapping of wild cattle and mustang horses. There was a duplicate of the town of Matador as it was in the beginning when it consisted of a postoffice, jail, saloon, and two or three stores.

The walls of the bunk house were decorated with scenes from various places on the Matador Ranch and pictures of fine horses and beautiful cowgirls. Along with these were some Western stories of a historical nature. You can imagine the delight it gave the author of this book when he found one of his own yarns on display in this museum of cowboy lore.

Several hundred over-age, wild, semi-longhorn steers were recovered from the "Bad Lands" of the Matador ranch in 1936. There probably will always be some wild cattle on the Matador Ranch, but fine registered bulls have been in general use for years. The company buys 20 or 30 fine registered Hereford bulls at the Denver, Omaha, and Fort Worth livestock shows each year. These are mated to registered females on the ranch and help produce the registered bulls for the 45,000 head usually found in the commercial herd. The Matador registered herd is divided into three classes. At the top are the prize bulls and about 300 of the finest cows. These produce the bulls and cows for a larger registered herd. This herd then provides the registered bulls for the range cattle. As a result of this breeding procedure, Matador steers have become famous for their quality. Matador cattle averaged $150 per head for all cattle sold in 1950, compared to $123 on the the national average.

Twenty-five hundred choice steers sold in February of that year brought what newspapers hailed as a million dollar sale. The Matadors usually held their cattle during the periods of extreme price depression. These often went to market later at 4 or 5 years old and at good prices. In normal times, nearly everything goes through a feed lot and goes to market as prime beef. Many of the cattle are fattened under contract with northern feeders. The Matadors always have something ready to ship, and try to take advantage of any favorable market. The bulk of the stock goes to Chicago, but any sudden strength at Kansas City, Denver, Fort Worth, or Omaha will divert a shipment to those markets.

General offices of the Matador Land & Cattle Co. were established in Denver in the early days of the ranch and were never changed. This was adjacent to a good market and about half way between the breeding grounds in Texas and the finishing pastures in Montana and the Dakotas. Home offices remained at Dundee, Scotland, until sale of the ranches to American interest in 1951. The Matador headquarter buildings in Texas are located 3 miles south of the town of Matador, on a hilltop that gives a fine view of the ranch with its thousands of fine Herefords. The main building has much the appearance of a country club.

Murdo MacKenzie resigned as general manager in the 30ies after having worked cattle on three continents and after having spent some 60 years with the Matador herds. J. M. Reilly was manager of the home ranch at Matador during the drought of 1936. For assistant and bookkeeper, he had D. I. W. Birnie, who fought with the kilted Scotts known as the "laddies from hell" in World War I, one of the two men of his company said to have survived that terrible conflict with its poison gas.

Early in 1951 stockholders living in the United States received word from the home office in Dundee, Scotland, that a group of Americans had made an offer of $18,960,000 for the Matador ranches and that sale of the property would be considered at the meeting of stockholders April 15. There were 800,000 ordinary shares outstanding at that time. These shares which had a nominal value of five shillings or about 70 cents per share had advanced steadily through the years and were then selling on the London Stock Exchange at six pounds, three shillings, nine pence or $17.50 per share. About 77 per cent of the Matador stock was held by British owners. The remaining 23 per cent was American owned. Now they had an offer of $23.70 per share, or $6.20 more per share than the stock would bring on the open market. There was, also, considerable money in the company treasury that could be disbursed to further enhance the profit.

John MacKenzie, general manager for the company in the United States, and a few others were opposed to sale of the big ranches that had provided a steady income for its owners for 69 years and had advanced in value from 70 cents pershare to $23.70 a share. That the stock was held in big blocks was apparent from the fact that the meeting was attended by only 15 shareholders or proxies. Mrs. Edith Donovan of London, owner of 40,000 shares and largest Matador stockholder, was not present. All the original founders of the company were dead, and their successors were feeling the pinch of the post-war period, and they voted to sell, after reserving one half the oil rights. Most of the Alamocita division was already under lease to the Superior Oil Co. of California and the Matador home ranch was leased to Humble for development.

The stockholders unanimously approved Manager John MacKenzie's report and accounts and voted a final dividend of 20 per cent, together with a final bonus of 15 per cent, making with the interim dividend of 10 per cent and interim bonus of 5 per cent already paid, a total of 50 per cent for the year.

Wilfred James Sainsbury of London was named liquidator for the Matador stockholders. Lazard Brothers & Co., Limited, of London handled the sale.

Deeds filed in August revealed that the great Matador Ranch, with holdings of over 800,000 acres and 47,000 head of cattle were to be broken up into 15 smaller ranches, with Albert K. Mitchell, who had managed the 400,000 acre Bell Ranch in New Mexico for many years, playing a leading part in the history of the Matadors under its new ownership. Although the old Matador, with cattle truly on a thousand hills, has been reduced in size, it is still in the cattle business, with a lot of lusty sons and daughters following in its footsteps. Deeds show that the Pease River Cattle Corporation holds 65,358.4 acres and the Turtle Hole Cattle Corporation had 46,580.36 of the former Matador range. Other members of the Matador family are just as vigorous. With improved pastures, better livestock breeding, and the prospects for oil, any one of these may someday equal the old Matador on the day when it sold for $18,960,-000.

CHAPTER X.

JOHN T. McELROY AT THE FOOT OF THE PLAINS

Ranching Where "God Ain't No Cowman"

Marketing of the cattle has always been one of the big problems of the ranchers. Those who solved it well became wealthy while those who depended on the ordinary markets made slow progress or went broke. In the days before the building of the railroads, John S. Chisum made a fortune by fighting his way through hostile Indian country and selling beef to the United States Army in the field against the savages. It was a risk that only a few cattlemen cared to take.

Capt. Richard King solved the marketing problem of the early days by building up his ranch on the Gulf Coast of Texas where the cattle could be shipped by water. At the time of his death he had 500,000 acres of land. His descendants, building on the firm foundation he laid, increased the holdings until the King ranch contained more than 1,000,000 acres.

John T. McElroy of the Odessa country at the foot of the Staked Plains in Texas solved the marketing problem by establishing a meat packing plant at El Paso, Texas, where he could sell his beef in both the United States and Mexico.

This great cattleman was born in Clinton County, Ohio, in 1849, the exciting year of the California gold rush; and his career has been as varied and thrilling as the year of his birth. John T. McElroy inherited the aggressive, pioneer spirit of his father who made the trip to California in a prairie schooner and returned by way of the Isthmus of

Panama. Following in the footsteps of his father, John T. McElroy, too, went to California after the Civil War. He did not find a gold mine, but he did discover that a fortune could be made from rapidly multiplying herds if properly marketed. He made his first cattle deal in Eugene, Oregon, where he bought a small herd from a man named William Miller.

An attack of cowboy fever succeeded that of the gold fever; and McElroy went to Texas, the home of the American cattle industry, and became a trail driver. In this employment he helped to drive herds to the end of the railroads in Kansas and to new ranches in the Far North. While other cowboys spent their wages in grand sprees at the towns at the end of the railway, McElroy became known as "Titus" and saved his hard earned coin for the day when he would start a ranch of his own somewhere on the broad prairies of the Southwest.

As his capital increased, he began to drive cattle for himself. On one of these drives, he bought a herd at Guaymas, on the west coast of Mexico, and drove them to Dodge City, Kansas, a journey of approximately 2,000 miles. The cattle were the long legged, lank type introduced into Mexico from the dry, hot plateaus of the Iberian peninsula. What they lacked in beef qualities they made up for in ability to furnish their own transportation.

Traveling a few miles a day, the Chihuahuas toiled over the mountain and vast prairies of Mexico. At times great desert plains unfolded to view with purple mountains rising on their confines. Often the only vegetation was a fringe of stunted shrubs that grew along the arroyos and dry streams that descended from the mountains to lose themselves in the sandy waste. For days there were no signs of habitation save perhaps a distant cloud of dust that marked the course of some peon's ox cart or a *vaquero*. There were vast flats of cacti and thorny shrubs that raked the tough hides of the Chihuahuas and plucked at the boot-tops of the cowboys. Eddying whirlwinds wound their irregular courses across the desert plains. There was lots of big game in the mountains; but on the desert, only a few prairie dogs and jackrabbits were to be seen. The sun rose and set, making its glowing arc across a cloudless sky.

The desert of northern Mexico, although hot through the day, became cool and beautiful at night; and there were many long, moonlight drives when they were in a region of little water.

The first part of the journey lay through the Yaqui Indian country. This tribe had fought the Spainards and Mexicans since the days of the exploration and were still partially unsubdued. McElroy employed some of the young Yaquis as guides and cowboys and thus secured a friendly passage through their region.

The cattle were driven northeast to Nogales, Arizona, on the Mexican border. From there they went east along the Border to Ft. Hancock on the Rio Grande and then to the Pecos near historical Horse Head crossing. Here they struck John Chisum's trail that led up the Pecos and across the Panhandle of Texas to Dodge City. It took three years to make the journey. At the end of the trip, McElroy's cattle had increased in number and weight and had tripled in value. Calves born on the trail had become large animals.

McElroy's first ranch was on the green meadows of the Gulf Coast south of San Antonio, the original home of the Texas longhorn. There, under the warm, moist breeze of the Gulf, the grass grew knee high and was green almost the year around. Mosquitos and the fever tick, however, were a serious drawback; and after eight years in that locality, McElroy went to the Nueces River 60 miles below Uvalde. Later he went to the Trans-Pecos country and established one of the largest cow pastures in the state. After the roundup, McElroy would drive his cattle to Kansas. Neighboring ranchers often turned their cattle over to him to market on a commission. These would be thrown with his own stock and driven to Dodge or other markets.

The rainfall in the Trans-Pecos country was light, and there were times when drought rode the range, leaving decimated herds and parched pastures in its wake. At times like this, starving, thin flanked cattle gathered around dryed up water holes and bawled their protest until death ended their misery. The only things that flourished were the buzzards and coyotes that grew fat on the great caron feasts.

Sometimes McElroy moved his cattle up on the Staked Plains or crossed the Rio Grande into Mexico. This was done only as a last resort, however, for cattle that are moved keep trying to go back to their old range; and the loss by straying is considerable.

The grass was a little better at the foot of the Staked Plains east of the Pecos, and McElroy went to the Odessa region and gradually built up a large ranch there. The blizzards that sometimes swept across the Staked Plains usually played out or decreased in severity by the time they reached the McElroy cattle; and although the range there was often dry and parched, McElroy made some money.

It is said that during one of the numerous drought a cowboy rode in from the east pasture one evening with the information that the water holes were drying up and that the grass was almost gone.

"Well, Ben," replied the rancher, "maybe the Lord will send us some rain after a while."

"I hope so, Boss. But if he don't send it soon, he ain't no cow man," was the reply.

It was in 1919 while operating his Odessa ranch that John T. McElroy conceived the idea of establishing a meat packing plant to dispose of his beef. He had just shipped some good steers to El Paso and had failed to sell them at a reasonable price. It was the same old problem that had kept so many cattlemen down. With the help of Ed R. Ardoin, Jr., and two laborers McElroy founded the El Paso Packing Co. Ardoin became manager of the packing house. This young West Texan was born at Pecos where he learned all about cattle on the range. Later he worked in the stockyards at El Paso and then in a butcher shop in that city. McElroy and Ardoin both had to struggle, but they knew their business and prospered.

Their first plant was an old rented cooler. In the beginning only cattle from the McElroy ranches were slaughtered. As the meat packing business grew, the ranches and feed lots were enlarged. The ranches could not keep up with the growth of the meat packing, however, and McElroy and Ardoin began to buy cattle, sheep, and hogs on the El Paso market.

In 1927 oil was discovered on McElroy's Odessa ranch near the south end of the Staked Plains. The financial worries of the cattleman were now definitely over.

The meat packing business had become a substantial business, supplementing the great wealth that oil brought. In 1933 the name of the company was changed to the John T. McElroy Packing Co., and a new plant costing $150,-000 was erected at 3800 Rosa Street. It was modern, complete, and designed to meet rigid government regulations. The building was lined with cork throughout to aid in refrigeration. The plant had a capacity of 288 beeves and 480 hogs a day. The meat was distributed throughout the Southwest in especially designed refrigerator trucks.

Animals were driven from the pens to the slaughter rooms through long chutes with the use of electric poles. Cattle were knocked in the head, bled, and then skinned while suspended from shackles. After the hogs were killed, they were dumped into big vats of boiling water to loosen the hair. An electric de-hairing machine was one of the modern features of the plant. Cattle were skinned by hand. The hides were salted and shipped to market in car load lots. Nothing whatever was wasted. Even the blood was cooked, dried, and sold for hog feed and fertilizer.

The packing house was equipped with huge fire pits for smoking and curing meat. There was a sun porch for sunning and airing, pickle vats, mixers, and grinders. There were sterilizers for the knives and other equipment, and workmen cleaned their hands in washing machines.

The plant was cooled by two 15-ton refrigerator machines. A separate building for the federal inspector was erected. The government inspection services is designated to eliminate all unfit meat from the food supply. It goes farther and sees that preparation of the meat is done cleanly. No harmful dyes of chemicals are allowed to be used. As in all federal inspected plants, no false or misleading statements or labels are allowed. All packing houses that do an interstate business are required to have this federal inspection, as provided by the meat inspection act of June 30, 1906, and supplementary legislation. This law grants qualified exemption to retail dealers and meat slaughtered on the farm. Each packing house is given a federal inspection number, and the source of any piece of meat can be determined by reference to the inspection stamp.

Animals are examined before they are slaughtered, and the meat is inspected when it is dressed. All condemned animals had to be disposed of outside of the plant. After the stock was butchered, the inspector examined the carcass and organs for any defect that could not be seen when the animal was alive. Each cut of meat was then stamped with the official inspection stamp. In the McElroy plant, as in all federal inspected plants, only meat fit for human consumption was passed by the inspectors.

At the time of his death in 1936, Mr. McElroy had disposed of most of his property at the foot of the Staked Plains, but he still had four ranches in New Mexico and Texas. These were furnishing about 70 per cent of the cattle slaughtered in the $150,000 plant in El Paso. W. C. Simpson was in charge of the business in El Paso and elsewhere. He, too, was a real cowman, a product of the Staked Plains. He was raised in Crosby County, Texas, making his first trip up the trail in the '90s. A cowboy of unusual business acumen, he finally became treasurer of this meat packing company that sold its products in both the United States and Mexico.

CHAPTER XI.

WILLIAM H. BONNEY ALIAS BILLY THE KID

A Cowboy Gunman at the End of the Trail

Although the Tunstall Ranch for which Billy the Kid worked was in the rough country west of the Pecos River in New Mexico, the Staked Plains became the refuge of the youthful gunman when he was driven out of Lincoln County, New Mexico.

The cowboy was only 18 years old when Governor Lew Wallace stopped the great cattle war in Lincoln County, New Mexico, by issuing a proclamation of amnesty to all except Billy the Kid and J. J. Dolan, surviving leaders of the opposing fighting forces in the cattle war. These two were ordered to stand trial for their crimes, while their followers were told to return to peace and quietness or be arrested by cavalry of the U. S. Army. Dolan had surrendered, stood his trial, and was acquitted. The Kid, however, had made so many enemies while fighting for Tunstall, Chisum, and McSwain that he did not believe he could lay aside his weapons and lead a quiet life. His chances for escaping punishment in court were no doubt slim. When he failed to surrender and take the consequences, the way was left open for his arrest and prosecution.

When the fighting ceased and most of the cattlemen went back to their ranching, Billy the Kid Bonney went out onto the Staked Plains east of the Pecos and got a job in the vicinity of Portales Spring. Governor Wallace was inclined to be lenient with the youth if he would stop his gun work; but men who had opposed the Kid clamored for action against him, so officers went after the chief gunman of the cattle war. Bonney made his escape, crossed the Texas line, and went up to the north end of the Staked Plains. He hung around Old Tascosa, where no one bothered him. He had a sweetheart at Ft. Sumner, N. Mexico, however, and returned to the town on the Pecos for visits. He was wanted for killing Sheriff William Brady and others during the Lincoln County War and was accused of stealing cattle.

At Tascosa, the Kid was joined by Tom Pickett, Tom O'Folliard, Dave Rudabough, and Charlie Bowdre. Some of these had been comrades of Billy the Kid during the cattle war. Others were notorious gunmen with indictments against them. The Kid was younger and smaller than any of the men who had collected around him. He had a slender, compact, boyish figure with sloping shoulders, dark brown hair, and blue eyes. He was 5 feet 8 inches tall and weighed 140 pounds. It was his small, well-shaped hands that had established him as the quick-draw man of the Southwest. He wore his pistol on his left side and fired with deadly aim with his left hand. This left his right free to handle the Winchester he usually carried. The Kid and his men rode good horses and were constantly on the lookout for matched races.

There were no complaints against the man in Texas. Officers at Tascosa gave them no trouble while they helped with the roundups or amused themselves by gambling and dancing. Bonney was never accused of robbery, and there is little to prove that he stole any large amount of stock. Jim East, chief deputy sheriff at Tascosa, and John W. Poe, deputy United States marshall, kept their eyes on the wild cowboys that had been driven out of New Mexico but found nothing that would justify their arrests, which was almost certain to result in bloodshed.

During his first term of office, Pat Garrett, sheriff of Lincoln County, New Mexico, received instructions to kill or capture Billy the Kid if he returned to the state. Bonney was at that time somewhere in the vicinity of Tascosa. When December, 1880, rolled around, Charlie Bowdre sent word to his wife at Ft. Sumner that he had the Kid were returning to the town on the Pecos to spend Christmas. This was news too good to keep. She told some friends. The information reached Barney Mason, Pat Garrett's brother-in-law and deputy sheriff at Ft. Sumner. Mason passed the word on to Garrett at Lincoln, and a trap was laid for Billy the Kid. Deputy Sheriff Jim East came down to the town on the Pecos a few days ahead of Bonney with full information as to the strength of the Kid's party and stayed to help kill or capture him.

Not knowing that officers were waiting at Ft. Sumner, Bonney and his friends crossed the Staked Plains and approached the town. At the edge of the residential section, Billy the Kid turned off the road and proceeded alone toward the home of his sweetheart. Pickett, O'Folliard, and Bowdre continued toward the business section. The officers were crouching in the shadow of a building when they heard the sound of hooves on the road that descended from the Staked Plains. O'Folliard was riding in advance when Sheriff Pat Garrett suddenly raised up and, with cocked rifle, ordered the men to halt and "put em up!" All went for their guns, and Garrett fired. O'Folliard was shot through the stomach and almost knocked from his horse by the impact of the bullett. Clutching at his saddle and screaming with agony, he slid from his horse. The posse fired at the others, but they escaped in the darkness. O'Folliard died before morning and was buried in the old military cemetery east of town.

At the sound of the first shot, Billy the Kid wheeled his horse around and raced to rejoin his men. Finding that they were badly outnumbered, they retreated toward the Staked Plains and took refuge in an abandoned stone house at

Stinking Springs. They were discovered by a neighboring rancher who sent word to the officers. The following night the officers surrounded the house. Soon after daylight, Charlie Bowdre came out with morrals to feed the horses. As he was adjusting one of the nose bags, he stopped and shouted something to the men inside the house. Believing they were discovered, the officers opened fire. Bowdre reeled and staggered but reached the door. Seeing that he was badly wounded and could not live long without medical care, Bowdre came out an hour later and surrendered. He was already dying, however, and death came before he could be removed to Ft. Sumner.

The horses stood by the side of the house where the wall protected them from the winter wind. Billy the Kid got a pole, and without exposing himself, caught his mount and led him inside the house. As soon as night came, he hoped to make a dash for freedom. When Dave Rudabough tried the same thing, Garrett shot the horse so that he fell and blocked the only door to the hut. From the shelter of an arroyo, the officers began shooting at the ropes that held the remaining horses. They did not have much luck in cutting the ropes but succeeded in frightening the animals so that they broke loose. The men inside the house now had only one mount and little chance to get him out the door. With two of their comrades dead, and outnumbered four to one, Pickett and Rudabough proposed that they surrender. Billy the Kid begged them to stick with him until night, when they would have a chance to shoot their way out.

The ranch house was of stone and formed an excellent defense. The sheriff ordered his men to remain under cover and fire only when someone appeared at the door or windows. A few shots were exchanged without damage to either party.

Before the day was over, the drinking water and fire-wood gave out. There was not a chance to get food, and little prospect for escaping. In the shelter of the arroyo, Garrett and his men cooked and ate a hot meal while Bonney and his men shivered within the bleak walls of the Mexican hut. The luck that had favored the youth during the cattle war had failed him when he became an outlaw. He might have tried to hold out until darkness but the only avenue of escape was a single door with a dozen guns trained on it. A parley was held, and the Kid and his two remaining companions surrendered on condition that they be protected from mob violence and given a fair trial. Bowdre's body was taken back to Ft. Sumner for burial.

Not wishing to stir up the smoldering embers of the cattle war, Garrett started to Santa Fe with the prisoners, traveling by way of Las Vagas. Not long before, citizens of the "Meadow City" had posted notices warning the Kid and other undesirable characters to leave town and to prove they meant it, had hanged two on the cross-bar of the well in the plaza when they ignored the request. Although the wild cowboy had returned against his will, many thought he would look good dangling from the same public watering place.

When the threat of the crowd became serious, the Kid asked for a gun, saying that he could "lick the whole dam outfit." He said he would not use the weapon against the sheriff and would surrender when the fight was over if he was still alive. Garrett had promised to protect the cowboy, and he had no intention of allowing him to be mobbed. He told the crowd that he would give Bonney his arms if they persisted. The prospects of facing the notorious gunman equipped to shoot it out cooled the ardor of the mob, and the officer was allowed to proceed with his prisoner.

Bonney was tried before Judge Warren Bristol on charges of having killed Bernstein, clerk at the Mescalero Indian Agency. The Kid still had both friends and enemies in Lincoln County, and when court opened the excitement became intense. So serious was the situation that the judge was afraid to stay at the county seat. He took lodging with the military forces at Ft. Stanton and rode over each day under military escort. The sheriff was instructed to search every person entering the court room. Many revolvers were collected the first day. Even the attorneys were found to be heavily armed. Under these conditions, Bonney's case was removed to Mesilla on the Rio Grande.

The Kid was without funds, and the court appointed Ira W. Leonard of Lincoln to defend him. Bonney proved that he had been attacked by Bernstein and others and had fought the clerk in self defense. He was acquitted. The prosecution did not stop there, however. The cowboy was immediately tried for the slaying of Sheriff William Brady. He could not claim self defense against an officer, and he was convicted. He was taken back to Lincoln to be hanged.

While awaiting execution, Billy the Kid was secured with leg irons and handcuffs. An armed guard stood over him day and night. The cowboy appealed to Governor Wallace to commute his sentence to imprisonment, but the governor delayed. A short time before the day of execution, a deputy named Bell was guarding Bonney. Jailer Olinger took the other prisoners across the street to dinner, and Bell and the Kid were left alone playing cards. In those days, guns were a very interesting subject; and Bonney began to tell Bell about a pearl handled, double action revolver he had taken from Brady the day he killed the officer. The cowboy said that he had been afraid to carry such incriminating evidence and had hid the gun in a hollow tree on the road to

White Oaks. He offered to make a map so Bell could find the pistol if he wanted it.

This choice weapon was certainly something to be prized, and the officer hastened to bring pen and paper so Bonney could clearly indicate its location. Billy the Kid labored at the drawing but was having difficulty because of the handcuffs.

"Wait a minute, Kid, and I will take those things off," Bell said. With this he unlocked the hand cuffs.

Bonney finished the map and handed it to the officer. The jailer looked at it and began to ask questions. Billy the Kid began to point out things on the map. When close to the officer, that deadly left of the cowboy moved. The chief gunman of the Lincoln County war had made many quick draws, but he probably never made a faster one than when he pulled Bell's gun. The guard upset a chair and scattered the cards as he whirled and found himself covered with his own pistol.

Marching Bell before him, the Kid limped down the hall toward the arms room, his leg chains making progress slow. The officer made a sudden plunge for the stairs, believing the leg irons would handicap the cowboy sufficiently for him to make his escape. Moving both feet at the same time, the Kid reached the head of the stairs in a few great leaps and sent a bullet through the back of the fleeing officer. Bell fell mortally wounded. Seizing a double barrel shotgun, Bonney hastened to a window. Jailer Olinger had rushed into the street with drawn pistol. Looking up, he called, "Bell! Oh, Bell! Did you kill the son of a b---?"

"Yes. And now I am going to kill another yellow cur," the Kid said, and shot the jailer with a load of buckshot. Several citizens saw Olinger fall. They now hastened to get back indoors. Many still sympathized with the Kid, and others reasoned that battling the worst gunman in the Southwest was purely a task for experienced officers.

Several horses were hitched in front of the courthouse and along the street. The Kid caught and mounted one of the best of these. He still wore the leg irons, and he had to ride sideways like a woman. The horse, like many cow ponies, promptly started pitching; and Bonney was thrown off. He held onto the reins, got up, mounted again, and, holding the horse's head high so he could not buck, galloped out of town.

He turned into the heart of the Capitan Mountains. He soon reached the hut of a friendly Mexican. There, with the aid of an ax and a hammer, he cut off the leg irons. He was now free, but the Kid knew Sheriff Pat Garrett, who was out of town when he escaped, would soon be on his trail. He rode on a few miles. Then he took the bridle off the horse he was riding and turned it loose. While Garrett was trailing the roving horse, the Kid made his way to the Block ranch on foot. Friends there provided him with a good mount, and he made his escape to the Pecos.

For a time the sheriff lost all trace of the youthful outlaw. Many thought he had gone to Mexico. In July, 1881, a rumor reached Garrett that the Kid was back on his old stamping ground at Ft. Sumner on the Pecos River. John W. Poe, deputy United States Marshal, had obtained the information from a man at White Oak, a mining town north of the Capitan Mountains. Garrett placed little faith in the report but proceeded to investigate. Bonney, with a death sentence over him, was now alone and was forced to spend most of his time in hiding.

Three good men went after the cowboy. They were Patrick F. Garrett, sheriff and former buffalo hunter; Tip McKinney, deputy and Indian fighter; and John W. Poe, deputy

U. S. Marshal, and former city marshal of Fort Griffin, one of the toughest places in Texas.

The officers traveled at night and lay concealed in the canyons during the day for fear that the Kid would hear of their approach. When within a few miles of the town on the Pecos, Garrett and McKinney concealed themselves and sent Poe, who was not known at Ft. Sumner, to scout around. Riding into town, Poe explained that he was a miner from White Oaks and was on his way back to Texas. He tried to draw several persons into conversation in regard to the Kid, but they shut up like clams when the youth was mentioned. Unable to learn anything at Fort Sumner, Poe went to see M. Rudolph, a justice of the peace who lived about ten miles from the town. Rudolph told Poe nothing, but he was so alarmed by the officer's visit that Poe became convinced that Billy the Kid was in that vicinity. The Justice of the Peace was probably afraid Bonney would learn of the officer's visit and suspect him of aiding Garrett.

Confident the Kid was in that locality, Poe rode by night to a place where he had agreed to meet Garrett and McKinney. The officers then decided to watch the home of the cowboy's sweetheart. They concealed themselves in a peach orchard back of the house and watched until 11 o'clock. Seeing no sign of Bonney, they decided to question Pete Maxwell, a prominent citizen of Fort Sumner.

Going to the Maxwell house, Garrett went inside to talk to the owner while Poe and McKinney remained on guard on the outside. Maxwell was in bed. Rousing him, the officer said:

"Pete, this is Garrett. We are after Billy the Kid. We know he is in Ft. Sumner. Will you tell us where he is?"

Maxwell replied, "Garrett, you and the Kid are both friends of mine. I want to be square with all my friends; I, therefore, am not taking sides with either of you."

Poe sat down upon the front porch, and McKinney loitered in the shadow at the side of the house. While Garrett was inside talking to Maxwell, Poe saw a young man come from a house across the street and approach the Maxwell residence. The officers supposed the fellow was some member of Maxwell's family or one of his sheep herders. Just as the visitor stepped upon the porch, he discovered Poe. The United States Marshal had beat many quick draws, but he did not have a chance with the lightning-like movements of the visitor. Before he knew it, Poe was looking down the barrel of a pistol and realized too late that he was face to face with Billy the Kid. Afraid of killing some member of Maxwell's family, the Kid hesitated to fire and demanded, "Who is it?"

Just then McKinney rose from the shadow at the side of the house. Billy the Kid backed into the door of Maxwell's room and again called in Spanish, "Quien es?"

Expecting to be killed at any instant and wishing to stall for time, Poe answered, "No one who will hurt you."

This partially satisfied the cowboy, and he turned to Maxwell and asked, "Who are those men, Pete?"

Coming into the darkness of the room from the moonlight, the Kid did not see Garrett. The cowboy, however, had on a white shirt and was distinguishable in the light of the open door. The sheriff had recognized the voice of the Kid. The cowboy heard the click of Garrett's pistol as the officer cocked the weapon. Like a cat at bay, the Kid whirled and faced the sound with his own gun cocked. Still fearing that he might kill some member of his friend's family by mistake, he did not fire. Garrett's pistol flashed. Maxwell let out a yell and plunged headlong through a window. Outside, he narrowly escaped being killed by Poe. Just in time the officer saw the difference between the man in night clothes and the cowboy who had entered the room. There was another shot, and Garrett came through the window close behind Maxwell.

The officer made a dash for shelter. From protected positions, they called upon Bonney to surrender. There was no reply. They listened. All was silent. Garrett had fired twice and had escaped without injury. Dead shot that the Sheriff was, it was not likely that he had missed. After a time, the officers cautiously approached the room. Working along the wall, Garrett hung his hat on the barrel of his pistol and partially exposed it before the window, but there was no response from the gun of Billy the Kid. A candle was lighted, fastened to a pole, and raised to the window sill. Still there was no sound. It was possible that Bonney was waiting for an officer to show his head. An old Mexican woman, one of Maxwell's servants, calling on the Kid not to shoot her, ventured to look into the room. There the candle revealed the youthful cowboy dead. Garrett had shot him through the heart. The officer's second shot had missed and gone through a washstand.

Justice of the Peace Rudolph was summoned from Sunnyside, and an inquest was held. The sheriff was thanked for having rid New Mexico of the desperado. The cowboy was 21 years old when he was slain, and it was said that he had killed a man for every year that he had lived. The body was turned over to the native Mexicans who laid it to rest beside those of his slain comrades, Tom O'Folliard and Charlie Bowdre.

Chapter XII.

W. L. HYATT OF THE 22 OUTFIT

Eluding Comanches and Buffaloes on the Staked Plains

"What would you do if you had your rope on an elephant and couldn't hold him?" This question was asked by W. L. Hyatt as we sat in the lobby of the Spur Hotel and talked of the day he roped a buffalo bull. The subject of the buffalo had come up when I asked the cowboy who rode the Staked Plains in Indian days if he had ever roped anything he couldn't hold.

"I guess I would turn him loose," I replied.

"That's just what I did," said Uncle Bill, and he continued to spin the interesting tale which follows.

You see I came to the Staked Plains in 1878 with a herd that belonged to the 22 outfit. That was two or three years after the big fights with the Comanches on Blanco Canyon and the Tule just above here, and there were still a few scattered bands roving the plains and the rough country along the Caprock. We followed the Mackenzie trail right up to the Caprock and turned Hensley longhorns loose on what later became the Spur and Matador range.

The Hensleys were called the 22 outfit because of their brand. Jim Hall came a little later and established the Spur ranch here, which is now one of the divisions of the SMS and owned by the Swensons.

There was no one in the country except Indians and buffalo hunters when we came. The cottonwoods along the draws were full of wild turkeys, and we soon became tired of them. A cow man likes beef, you know. The Hensleys were rather stingy with their beef, however; and we ate buffalo calves. Some writers have left the impression that the buffalo went north and south like geese with the change

—136—

of the season. This may have been true farther north, but they stayed along the sunny eastern slope of the Caprock all the year. We could get a young, tender, milk-fed buffalo calf nearly any time we wanted him. There were a half dozen parties hunting buffalo for their hides in this part of the country. They worked much like a cow outfit. One or two dead shots did the shooting. Others did the skinning, while a third part of the crew took care of the meat, and others did the hauling of the hides to Ft. Griffin.

Those who cured the meat dug long trenches and lined them with buffalo hides, the flesh part up. The meat was removed from the bones in large chunks and placed in the trenches to take the salt. Later it was thrown out on the clean prairie sod to dry.

There were lots of bear here, too. One night I was standing guard to see that Indians did not take our scalps while we slept when I saw something that looked like a Comanche on his hands and knees. We always slept in a circle like the spokes of a wagon wheel with our heads to the center where they would not be convenient for a tomahawk, so I gave the wagon boss a kick on the foot to arouse him. When he was awake, we watched the thing coming up on all-fours. It would move forward a few yards, stop and listen. Then it would sneak up a little closer. I was about to shoot my first Indian when the boss said: "Bill, that ain't no Indian. It's a bear. It's too black for a Comanche."

Sure enough, is was a black bear. We watched to see what he would do. He came up and ate the scraps where the boys had emptied what was left on their plates. Then he went over and smelled the feet of one of the sleeping punchers. I guess he didn't like the odor, for he hurried off.

We built a dugout on the head of the Brazos at the edge of the Plains and laid in a supply of buffalo meat for the winter. Our boss, J. H. Hensley, left five of us there to look after the cattle and went back to Jacksborough for the winter. He had not been gone long when Indians came and stole every horse we had. One broncho got away and came back, and we drew straws to see who should take the horse and go for help. It was a 200 mile trip through a country infested with Comanches, and it fell to me!

I took a little dried buffalo meat for food and set out on the perilous journey. The other men barricaded themselves in the dugout. I tried to slip away so if there were Indians watching they would not get me. The first day, I rode until dark, hid my horse in a ravine, went off a quarter of a mile and slept under a cliff. I approached my horse very cautiously the next morning, fearing that Indians might be watching for me to return.

The grass was poor, and my horse began to give out in a few days. I knew I would fall an easy victim if the Comanches discovered me. Fortunately, I ran into some buffalo hunters first and persuaded them to lend me a fresh horse. I finally reached the Hensley farm near Jacksborough safely. John and his wife were busy about the corral and saw me coming on a strange horse. Their first words were, "Are they all dead but you?"

I told them the men were all right when I left but that I did not know how long they could hold out. We rounded up the horses on the ranch and started back with a fresh *remuda*. We found the men watching from a hill-top near the dugout. They had not been molested.

A little later I saw the Indians capture a boy. W. C. Dockum, who came here in the 70's, had a store on Dockum Creek where he was trading with the buffalo hunters and a few cowboys. I loped over there one day to get some tobacco and was there when Indians appeared on the scene. When I saw the Comanches coming, I started to get on my horse and *vamoose*. Dockum said, 'Hyatt, if you get on that horse, I'll kill you. You have got to stay here and help defend my wife'. I stayed.

Another fellow outrode the Indians and came in a few jumps in the lead. The Parish boy had gone after the family milk cow. The Comanches turned aside to chase him. They captured the boy and carried him off. Knowing that a rescue party would soon be on their trail, they turned him loose the next day but kept his horse.

A little later while on a roundup on McDonald Creek I ran onto a big band of Indians and came near losing my scalp. I laid down on my old bronc and pulled my freight for the herd. Some of the boys came to my assistance, and there was a hot little fight before we retreated to the wagon. We saw several Comanches fall, but we did not lose a man ourselves. My horse had an arrow sticking in him. We had to throw him down and cut it out. The Indians did not follow us to the wagon, though.

It was in 1883 when I roped the buffalo. By this time the hunters had almost exterminated the animals for their hides. We were on a big roundup, and the boys were spread out on a drive for the cattle when a lone buffalo came out of a ravine. He went on with the stock for a while but kept threatening to bolt for freedom. As the drive narrowed near the meeting place, he started to go through our lines. We decided to rope and brand him just for the fun of it. When he made his dash for the hills, he came out by me. I got down my old rawhide and laid it on fair. The buffalo hit the end of the lariat going like an express train. He yanked my horse about ten feet and nearly unseated me. If you think a buffalo won't fight, just try tossing a twine on him. That old fellow got up with blood in his eye and came straight for me. He caught my bronc and ripped open his rump at the first charge. The nag left with the buffalo working his horns in his tail. A buffalo is lots faster than a cow, and he had us headed down hill. The boys began to laugh and yell, 'Stay with him, Hyatt! Stay with him,' but they made no effort to help. How could I stay with him and me in the lead? I got out my old Barlow and began to whittle on the riata. I surely was glad when I got that rope sawed in two and there was nothing to slow my old bronc down.

The buffalo went back to the hills. He was killed in a drive a few days later by another outfit. He was still dragging part of my riata.

I rode herd one night near Amarillo Lake when three saddle horses froze to death. They were hot animals the boys had been riding while fighting to hold the cattle together in the blizzard.

After leaving the Hensleys, I spent 16 years with the Matador outfit. I made two trips up the trail to Montana.

It took all summer. We just grazed the cattle through. The trail went out by way of Tascosa, Clayton, Pueblo, and Cheyenne. We usually left Texas in March and got back in July or August. We shipped back. Nothing but steers were taken to the North. I knew a fellow by the name of John Smith who spent 16 Fourths of July on the trail to Montana.

I quit the Matadors in 1895 and went into the livery stable business at Dickens. When the automobile put driving horses out of business, I opened the hotel here. I guess I will just continue on here at Spur until it is time to go kicking down the trail.

Chapter XIII.

CLAUDE JEFFERS AND "HIGH POWER"

Bronc Peeler for the Matadors

Old "TCH" had been an outlaw for ten years. Bob Haley, wagon boss for the Matador outfit, was the last man to try to ride him. When he got thrown, the sixty odd punchers of the ranch decided the horse could not be ridden.

Of course, the champion of the Matador tough string had worked up to his position by disposing of one puncher after another. He was probably just a promising novice when he tossed his first cowboy into a mesquite bush at the McDonald camp; but he was a horse that could take an education, and he improved with each new experience. Practice makes perfect, so by the time he got to the wagon boss the outlaw had already sent about half the Matador outfit sprawling in the dust.

Haley, the boss, didn't pay much attention to what the punchers said about the horse at first; but as the outlaw disposed of good riders one after the other, the foreman began to realize that here was an animal that called for his own superior horsemanship. If the boys had known that the boss was going to try "THC", there would have been a flock of men sitting on the fence the morning the foreman met his Waterloo. Haley, however, was not a man for show or display; and there was no one present but a puncher and the cook the day the boss brought the outlaw in from the horse pasture, tied up one foot, and put a saddle on him. After carefully tying the rowels of his "gal leg" spurs so they wouldn't slip, Haley swung to the saddle and turned

"THC" loose. The wagon boss need not have gone to so much trouble about the spurs, for the big bay, with a lot of mustang ancestry back of him, promptly kicked off the things that ripped his belly. He then proceeded to sun his side until the Matador foreman didn't know whether he was on the horse's back or under his belly. After tying some knots in his tail, and in Haley's neck, "THC" unloaded the boss into a water trough and went off toward the horse pasture kicking at the empty stirrups and trying to throw the saddle.

After that, "THC" had the run of the 420,000 acre Matador pasture and was referred to as the horse that could not be ridden. The outlaw did such a first class job that for several years no one dared dispute what he could do. But about 1900 a slender, wiry youth was employed to break horses for the Matadors. He, like "THC", improved with practice. As the years went by, Claude Jeffers, breaking from 50 to 500 horses a year, got to be something of a champion himself. He reached his highest efficiency the year he broke 580 horses and put them through nine saddles each with the help of only one assistant. After the Matador broncs had seen for the ninth time that they could not unload the man on their back, they were pretty well convinced of the futility of bucking; and they were turned over to the punchers to become useful cow horses.

As bronc after bronc, a lot of them from the tough string, went down before the 135 pound Claude Jeffers, men began to say the horses had never been born that the youth couldn't ride. When someone made a spiel like that, some of the older hands always reminded them of "THC", the horse that could not be ridden. In the course of time, the Matador outfit found that it had a bronc peeler who could ride anything with hair on it; at the same time, it had a horse that could not be ridden. Many wondered what would happen if the two ever met. It looked like the irrestible force meeting the immovable object. Anything might happen, but they could not say what.

Claude Jeffers did not press for a show-down with "THC", but he continued to clean everything else they put into the corral. The funny thing about his riding was that he never used spurs. Most of the boys considered themselves goners when a spur strap broke or when a tangle foot like "THC" kicked them off. When Jeffers got into the saddle he just seemed "growed there." When someone insisted on knowing how he did it, he said, "Just leave your body limber and hold tight with your legs. Catch the motion and roll with the motion of the horse. Hold a tight rein to steady yourself." It sounded simple, but riding bad horses without spurs was not as easy as it sounded.

Some times the company paid Jeffers so much per head for breaking broncs, usually $2.00 per year of age; and some times he was paid the usual wages of a cow puncher with a bonus for the more hazardous work he was doing. Lots of different plans can be tried out in 37 years. That's how long Claude Jeffers broke broncs for the Matadors, an outfit that worked from 60 to 75 punchers and that still branded 10,000 calves a year as late as 1950.

Of course, when one has to break a large number of horses, he does not have time to train them; but Claude Jeffers was a horse trainer as well as a bronc peeler. In fact, it was his ability to turn out good horses as well as his qualifications to ride bad ones that made him indispensable to the great ranch. Jeffers proved what he could do. In 1935 his horse, "High Power", won first place and was pronounced the best cutting horse in the state of Texas at the Texas Cowboy's Reunion at Stamford. Jeffers entered this horse three years in succession in the cutting contest, and each year he took a prize and showed progress. The first year, "High Power" took third place. The second year he advanced to second, and the third time he took first. Jeffers rode him and carried off the $150 saddle offered as first prize.

"Horses are among the most intelligent animals in the world," says Claude Jeffers. "He can see better than a man at night; and his ears, movable in all directions, can detect sounds that man cannot hear. He can smell almost as good as a dog and often smells of his master to see if he is the right person if a change of clothes makes him appear different. Horses, like most people, can be handled best with kindness."

That is one reason this bronc peeler did not use spurs. You have to be a real horseman to ride a bad one without long shanks, but even the worst will pitch harder if he is lifted up on a pair of stickers every time he hits the ground.

"If you want to gentle a horse, be gentle," says Jeffers. "That's the whole secret. A nervous, fractious man makes a horse jumpy and hard to manage. Be good to a horse, and he will learn to love you like a dog. Some are temperamental just like people; but they love to work cattle, play polo, or run after hounds. I can ride "High Power" into a herd, show him a calf or a steer, take off the bridle, and he will do the rest. A man riding him might wonder whether he was coming or going, but out of the herd the cow critter will come."

It takes about the same thing to make a good cow horse as it does to make a good polo animal - sense, activity, and endurance. A cow horse should be heavier than a polo animal if there is much roping to be done. It takes a heavy horse to throw a heavy steer. They have some pretty big ones down on the Matador Ranch at the eastern edge of the Staked Plains. Ed D. Smith, one of the Matador cowboys, got one out of the Croton Breaks in the 30's that was 21 years old and had a horn spread of 42 inches. You see, the Matadors date all their cattle when they brand them; and it is easy to tell their exact age. The age is branded on the left shoulder; for example, in 1947 it was a 7. The regular Matador brand is a V on the left side. It looks like a 7-V, but it is not. It has been called a flying-V, but it is just a script V like you make when writing. The horse brand is 50 on the left hip.

Jeffers thinks the Morgans make the best cow horses. They are about the right weight for the average man, and have lots of ginger and endurance, too. The Steeldusts also are fine. They are active and learn quickly. They can't stand as much hard riding as the Morgans, though, in the opinion of Claude Jeffers. They are a little too nervous and work themselves down too soon. "High Power" is half Morgan and half Steeldust.

"For good cow horses from range mares, I would say that a Morgan stallion would be the best bet," says Jeffers. "Some people find that Hamiltonian is all right when crossed with range stock."

"How about the Mustangs?" I asked.

"Most of them are too small, and they never get gentle. It takes a gentle horse to work cattle with efficiency. If you want to run a good horse to death, put him after a Mustang. Those things can run until the world looks level. Capture a big one, and get him broke, and you will never be afoot, though. They are hard to tame. I have seen them stand in the corral for days without so much as looking at the water trough. You have to wear the Mustangs out and kill them in breaking them. They are complete wrecks by the time they quit fighting. There were thousands of them on the Staked Plains and along the Caprock until stockmen killed them off to save the grass they ate."

Claude Jeffers liked a medium swell fork saddle. The one he used before winning the $150 prize saddle at Stamford was made by Schueitzner of Matador, Texas. He often used double cinches with a girts just tight enough to hold the saddle on. A single cinch is not enough for roping purposes; and it has to be made too tight for the best results in breaking bronchos, he believed.

"It's the tight cinches that tend to cut off a horse's breath that makes many of them buck so hard. They are much like a man fighting for air. They do not object to the weight on their backs as much as they do to being strangled. As for spurs, nearly any person is ticklish and will jump if suddenly poked in the ribs. A horse is the same way. He either starts pitching or tries to escape by flight," said the Matador bronc peeler.

Jeffers thought there was nothing as good as the Navajos for saddle blankets. They are soft but firm and do not scald a horse's back. A whole lot depends on the weave, but it is probably the natural wool that makes them so desirable. Army physicians long ago found that soldiers got along alright with woolen shirts, even in warm climates. Cotton tends to harden a blanket, and hair scratches too much. Wool keeps a horse warm in winter. In summer it collects the prespiration and provides a cooling process by evaporation, according to Jeffers.

Although Jeffers broke broncs for the Matadors for 37 years and converted over 3,000 young animals into cow horses, he was never permanently crippled. He was sometimes blue and black all over, but he was never hurt in a way that he did not get over it. On the other hand, Ed D. Smith, another Matador cowboy, has been thrown and kicked about so much that he has a shoulder that slips out of place with the least sudden movement. Even a sneeze will often throw out of place the shoulder that horses and steers have dislocated so many times.

"Have you ever been throwed?" I asked.

Claude Jeffers stared at me as though he could not comprehend my ignorance.

"Say! If you ever meet a bronc peeler who says he has never been throwed, you can just put it down then and there that he is not what he claims to be. I've been throwed more ways than a scrambled egg, but I have never seen a horse I couldn't ride. I don't get throwed very often, but I feel pretty lucky when I go two or three years without getting spilled. Things will just naturally go wrong once in a while. Yes, I rode old "THC", the outlaw that had not been ridden for ten years. I'll tell you about that after we eat."

We pulled rawhide bottomed chairs to the table at McDonald camp and mixed Ed Smith's sour dough biscuits with more conversation. It took a lot of questions to bring out information from this man who had ridden more broncs than any man in the world.

Jeffers thinks 4 years old is the best age to break a cow horse. They are at their best age at 8 to 10. Like men, it takes time for a horse to get experience and become thoroughly efficient. An animal begins to deteriorate at about 12, Jeffers believes.

"Ten horses make a full string on the Matador Ranch, although I have seen some men who could get more work out of 5 or 6 than others could out of a dozen. It all depends on the man. If you want to make a hit with the Matadors, take good care of your horses. The better horseman you are, the more good horses you will get. If you are a horse killer, the range boss will probably give you some sorry animals to kill off. Every new hand gets a lecture on the care of his horses when he starts to work for the Matador outfit," Jeffers explained.

In winter, the string is cut down to about three horses to each man on the Matador Ranch. These are fed and can do a lot more work per horse than the summer remuda, which is ridden on grass. Horse feeding has changed, too, in recent years. The Matador cow horses are now given a balanced diet consisting of corn, oats, kaffir, a little cotton seed meal, etc., as figured out by feed experts at experiment stations. This is a ground feed that saves a horse's teeth. Ground feed is more completely digested, too. Jeffers says this is good feed for all ordinary purposes. For maximum endurance, there is nothing like shelled corn, he believes. The grass season is from the last of April to December 1. Mares are never used for working cattle on the Matador Ranch.

"Rawhide makes the best hobbles. Manila rope is too hard and often skins a horse's legs," says Jeffers.

Thirty to 45 feet is about right for a good lariat, although some men can throw a 60 foot rope. For roping purposes, there is nothing better than Manila hemp. Riatas are all right when dry, in the opinion of the Matador bronc peeler.

Although Claude Jeffers was one of the greatest riders in the world, he seldom performed for rodeos. Peeling broncs for a real cow outfit is different from the showmanship of a rodeo. In the rodeo, the object is to thrill the audience. On the ranch, the purpose is to make a good cow horse. Jeffers was not spectacular, but everything he did was practical. Stunt flying is entertaining, but it is not the best method for winning a battle in the clouds.

The methods of the rodeo won't turn out champion roping or cutting horses like "High Power"; and the Matador outfit was paying their man to produce fine cow horses, not bad ones. Jeffers, without tricks or fancy stunts, would not have looked spectacular on a bad horse; but he could have kept his saddle just as long as any one. There is probably not a man living who can go out and put 580 young horses through nine saddles in a year. Max Bentley, special writer for the Ft. Worth Star Telegram, has called Jeffers the "champion bronc buster of the world." If the number of horses ridden counts, that is what he was.

There was a time when the Matador bronc peeler thought every horse had a certain number of bucks in him and proceeded to let him get them out of his system. Later he tried to discourage pitching ambitions. It is something they do not need to practice to become good cow horses.

Although Claude Jeffers disliked to ride for public appearance, he rode a few times for local people. For years the Matador punchers wanted to see him ride "THC", the horse that had cleaned about half the cowboys on the ranch. Jeffers finally agreed to ride him for the benefit of a local celebration that was about to go dead. When the news went forth that the man who could ride anything with hair on it was going to try the horse that could not be ridden, the cowboys and ranchers came in from all the range for 100 miles. There was the usual barbecue, calf and goat roping, and a lot of preliminary bronc busting before "THC" was finally eared down and saddled for Claude Jeffers. It had now been ten years since anyone had tried the famous outlaw.

The crowd held its breath as Jeffers swung to the saddle and said, "Let 'em go!"

The outlaw bogged his head and started to give his opponent the works. It had been ten years since old "THC" had thrown his last rider, and he may have forgotten a lot. Some of the old-timers who witnessed the contest were of the opinion that age had slowed the famous horse down. Others declared the outlaw did a first class job and that he just looked easy because it was Claude Jeffers who was in the saddle. It is reasonable to assume that the famous outlaw was at least badly out of practice. If "THC" remembered his former experience at all, he probably expected some demon to climb on his back and try to beat and strangle him to death. As he gave the saddle one violent shake after another, he may have discovered something different in this quiet boy who rode with a light, easy swing. No one beat him with a quirt nor gouged him with spurs. The saddle cinches were not tight enough to interfere with his breathing. After a moderate amount of hard pitching, the famous outlaw quit and trotted off without even making Jeffers show daylight.

Those who had bet on the horse were disappointed, and yelled for Jeffers to make "THC" strut his stuff. But Claude Jeffers played fair even with his horses, refusing to make mean horses out of those that wanted to be good. He patted "THC" understandingly, and sent him back to the Matador pasture.

Then someone in the crowd unhitched a mule famous for his cussedness, and drug him out for Jeffers to ride. This animal was in the prime of life and as full of Old Nick as a circus clown. The mule watched the saddling undisturbed and probably confident of his prowess. He had seen a good number of bronc peelers and had convinced them they were just ordinary cow hands. Jeffers may have looked to him just like another chap who should be made aware of the advisability of changing his profession.

When the bronc peeler landed on his back, Old Sam began to bawl and have wall-eyed fits. He rolled up until there wasn't anything 3 inches wide for the saddle to rest on. Jeffers stayed with the saddle and hoped that when it was over he would find a mule somewhere beneath. He couldn't tell just where the brute was while the fire-works were on. The mule bellowed and bawled. He fence rowed until the sky and earth became scrambled. The crowd got onto its feet and, with much laughter, hollered itself hoarse. Old Sam seemed to have more tricks in his bag than a magician. He hit the ground stiff legged, he whirled, and he sunned his side. The mule had a technique that differed somewhat from that of a horse. Jeffers had seen a lot of fancy steps, but that mule showed him some new ones. Old Sam had the wind of a buffalo bull and kept pouring it on thick and fast. The hard jar of his stiff leg jumps made the bronc peeler begin to hiccup. The saddle seemed to be tossed about in a hurricane. When the storm was over, Jeffers was still with the saddle; and there was an exhausted mule under it!

Claude Jeffers rode many bad horses in his 37 years as bronc peeler for the Matadors, a lot of them worse than either "THC" or Old Sam; but these two remain among the big surprises of his career. He was surprised at the ease with which he rode "THC", the horse he had once dreaded; and almost as much surprised that an ornery mule could pitch so long and display such a variety of tricks.

The hard jolting of the buckers is thought to have injured the famous bronc rider internally. He died at Matador in 1936 after having converted more broncs into good cow horses than any rider of the western range.

CHAPTER XIV

BOB CROSBY AND HIS CROSS-B RANCH

The World's Champion Cowboy

Many great cowboys have ridden the Western range, but to the Staked Plains goes the distinction of having produced the greatest cowpoke who ever forked a cayuse or wrapped up a cow critter. Just as the Llano Estacado had the largest ranch in the world, the XIT; just as it produced the world's largest steer, Slaughter's 4,000 pound animal; it likewise turned out the greatest of all the American rodeo performers, Robert Anderson Crosby.

This top hand, winner of the world's championship three times as the greatest all-round cowboy and permanent possessor of the Roosevelt Trophy, was the smiling, sun-tanned owner of the Cross-B ranch, 14 miles south of Kenna, New Mexico. He was proclaimed the greatest cowboy in the world because he could ride a rarin', sun-fishin' bronc and not pull leather, tie up a full-grown steer in a few seconds, and twist down the wildest longhorns ever turned loose at a rodeo.

Oklahoma and Arizona have tried to claim this genius of the Western range; but he was a product of the Staked Plains, with the honors divided between New Mexico and Texas. Robert Anderson Crosby, known to cow hands as "Bob", was born February 27, 1897, near Midland, Texas, at the south end of the Staked Plains. During the last 28 years of his life, he ran a spread near Kenna and Elida, New Mexico, in the west central part of the Staked Plains.

Bob Crosby's daddy, R. H. Crosby, was a cattleman and Texas Ranger. It is said that the elder Crosby played poker with one of his friends to see who should have first right to propose to Bob's mother. Be this true or not, there is plenty to prove that Bob got the very best of training in both moral conduct and the work of the range. He did not drink, chew tobacco, gamble, nor cuss. Even the proverbial sack of Bull Durham did not enter the shirt pocket of this top hand.

R. H. Crosby, Bob's father, was a member of Company D of the Texas Rangers, with headquarters at Ysleta on the Rio Grande. He made his first trip to New Mexico in 1881 when he went to the Socorro country after Jack Hunt and Howard Collier, wanted in Texas for murder and robbery. Crosby returned these prisoners to Fredericksburg, Texas, traveling by way of Lincoln, New Mexico, and John Chisum's ranch on South Spring River. He and another Ranger passed through Lincoln with their prisoners a few days after Billy the Kid had killed his jailers, Bell and Ollinger. They passed through Roswell without recognizing it, there being only four or five adobe houses there at the time.

R. H. Crosby became foreman of the NA ranch near Ft. Stockton, Texas. Later the family moved to Chelsea, Oklahoma, and lived in the same region as Will Rogers for 10 years. In 1918 the Crosby family went back to the Staked Plains and acquired a ranch of about 40,000 acres south of Kenna, New Mexico.

During the next five years, Bob Crosby and his brother, Harold, rode the range for their dad, chased wild steers through the prairie dog towns, and tossed their lariats in one of the windiest countries in the world. It takes a good roper to swing a lasso effectively in a sand storm and a first rate bronc to out maneuver a wild steer in a dog town. When Bob and his horse later hit the still atmosphere and smooth turf of the arena, it was like working cattle in paradise for both.

R. H. Crosby was a good roper and was often in the money at the rodeos at Roswell and other local places. When Bob got to be better than his dad, he had a lot of confidence in himself. Not all of his time was spent roping steers, for it was while riding the range at Kenna that he roped Miss Thelma Jones, daughter of Mr. and Mrs. W. B. Jones. He must have done a pretty good job of tying her up, because the knot was broken only by the death of the famous cowboy.

The Crosbys bought their cattle and ranch during the boom period of World War I. The slump that followed almost put them out of business. Bob tried working in the Oklahoma oil fields, but a cowboy removed from his horse is lost. Bob went back to his mount the first chance he had.

In the summer of 1923 Richard Merchant, another top hand, suggested that he and Bob go to New York City for the World Series rodeo. They agreed to split their earnings and hoped that at least one would be in the prize money. Bob borrowed $250 for expenses. Merchant took first prize in calf roping, and Bob got third money in the same event. Bob showed up well in so many other events, with seconds and thirds, that he got a contract to go with "Tex" Austin's cowboys to the British Empires Exhibition in London in 1924.

There were 165 cowboys and cowgirls in the party that sailed on the Menominee in June. Bob took his wife and 3-year-old daughter, Roberta, along. Roberta was the only child in the party, and she became the pet of the entire crowd. Bob also took his best roping horse, "Governor Brown."

At Wimbledon Stadium they met other cattlemen and expert horsemen from Canada, Australia, and New Zealand. Some opposition arose to the rodeo on the ground that it was cruel, and the King and Queen did not attend. The Prince of Wales came incognito. Most of the nobility practicipated enthusiastically, however, and urged on the contestants with exclamations of "Bravo!"

Approximately 100,000 persons passed through the turnstiles every day at the Exposition. Mrs. Crosby is not a cowgirl; and although she wore a ranch costume, she took little part in the rodeo. Roberta could already hold on to her daddy and ride better than some grown persons. She understood the roping, riding, and bulldogging and enjoyed it all except the steer wrestling. She was afraid her daddy would get hurt in this.

"Governor Brown" was 11 years old and at the height of his efficiency, and Bob expected to cop a lot of prizes with him. He often said: "There's nothing that horse can't do. I merely have to speak or sign and he obeys at once. Governor takes a delight in the rodeo, and seems to know instinctively what is wanted. He often thinks faster than I can."

Then Governor broke his leg on the second day of the rodeo. It was a tough blow to Bob. He bought another horse not near so good and went on. Crosby had roped only calves in the preceding rodeos, and he and his horse both had a lot to learn when they entered the steer roping at Wimbledon. The roping seemed to electrify the crowd. When Ad Eddins roped a steer and tied him in 37 seconds, there were excited cheers. Then when the cowboy from the Staked Plains roped a fleet animal and tied him up in 27 seconds the applause would have done credit to a Cup Final match. The world's record for steer roping at that time was 17 seconds. Although this was no where near his later performances, Bob took first money in steer roping at Wimbledon.

Sometimes the steers got on the prod and turned on the cowboys and there was a stampeed for safety from the lowered horns. Bob often let the stolid Britons in on a miniature bull fight when he flaunted a saddle blanket in the face of an enraged animal and let him gore it.

A lot of the Londoners thought ranching would be great sport until they saw the bulldogging and got the impression that it was all in the day's work. In this event, two horsemen race after the steer. The duty of one is to hold the animal on a straight course of flight while the other, the wrestler, gallops up along the left side, quits his saddle, and throws his weight on the steer's horns. The animal must be brought to a stop and thrown by twisting his neck. The cowboy digs his heels into the ground, comes down on the horns with a mighty twist and up on the nose, and man and beast rock and roll together. It is man's strength and skill matched against that of the bull. If the longhorn is the better of the two, he refuses to have his neck twisted and drags the cowboy around until he is exhausted. If the bulldogger has the power, the head of the brute is turned a little, then more, and finally the steer flops on his side, horns down, in order to prevent his neck from being broken. It is only a matter of seconds for men who hope to be within the prize money.

Bob made his best showing in roping. It was no small feat to place first in a steer roping contest with men from all over the world. Tom Webster, British cartoonist, drew a pretty little package wrapped and tied with the head and tail of a steer sticking out of it and labeled it: "Bob Crosby made a neat little parcel of his bull in 27 seconds."

There was an amusing little interlude one day. Representatives of nearly every British Colony and Dominion had gathered on the steps of the Canadian National Railway Pavalion and were having their pictures made when one of the wild American cowboys, riding at full speed and whooping and yelling like a drunk Indian, dashed up on his horse and took the central place in the group. It was Bob Crosby of the Staked Plains. Hindo Moguls and Canadian Mounties crowded around to have their pictures made with the American cowboy, his pretty wife, and little daughter. It might interest the "silver mounted" cowboys of the cinema to know that the picture shows that Bob Crosby was using a half inch rope for bridle reins.

Some of the bronc peelers went to the zoo for a ride on the camels and elephants. They found the camels so rough they had to pull leather. One of the elephants refused to let "Suicide" Elson on his back.

Julius Fleischmann, American millionaire, entertained about forty of the cowboys and cowgirls with a party. He had collected about half the smart people of London to meet them. The riders of the range came wearing their boots, ten gallon hats, and guns. The British were regular fellows, however, and got as much thrill out of it as the cow folks did. Lady Alexander danced with Charlie Winn; and Lady Maidstone, tall and Madonna-like, made quite a contrast with the bronzed young giant from the Purple Sage country. What the cowboys lacked in etiquette they more than made up for in sincere good manners. The conservative English folks relaxed and had such a good time that M. and Madame de Pena took the whole crowd to their lovely house on Hill Street for refreshments and more dancing when the place they were in closed. The London lady evidently knew her mavericks for the refreshments she served were bacon and eggs. The Britons thought the party great fun, and the cowboys and cowgirls went back to America with the impression that the English were a charming people. Bob went home with $3,000 in prize money. He often said that he could not have had more fun if he had been a millionaire.

Back in the United States, Bob Crosby began laying plans to win the Roosevelt Trophy and the world's championship as an all-round cowboy, the most prized award known to the cowboy world.

The Trophy was a silver horse and rider mounted on a globe of silver with the continents in gold. It was offered by the Roosevelt Hotel in New York City in memory of Theodore Roosevelt, the cowboy and Rough Rider who became President of the United States. It was awarded annually to the cowboy who could win the most events at the Cheyenne, Wyoming, Frontier Day Rodeo and the Pendleton, Oregon, Round-up. The Annual Trophies were of silver; and the big one had the continents in gold. It was offered to the cowboy who could win the world's championship three times. All the feats carried large cash prizes in addition to the $2,500 trophy. Most valuable of all to the follower of the rodeo was the title of World's Champion All-round Cowboy that went with the Roosevelt Trophy.

Yakima Cannutt of Yakima, Washington, had won it in 1923, the first year it was offered. Paddy Ryan of Ismay, Montana, had taken it in 1924.

Points toward the trophy had to be made in bronc busting, steer roping, or bulldogging. The contestant had to participate in at least two of these. Such an award tended to do away with men who were good in only one line. First place in the bucking contest carried 120 points; second place, 90; third, 60. Steer roping was counted the same. First place in bulldogging earned 100 points; second, 75; third, 50.

Bob had already demonstrated that he was one of the best steer ropers in the United States. He was also a near-champion in calf roping but this could not be counted in the world's championship.

On the home range, Bob had become known as "Wild Horse Bob" because of his riding ability. Bronc peeling, however, is the most dangerous of all cowboy feats; and Bob's wife begged him not to go into this. He chose steer bulldogging instead, no tame affair itself!

Bob took in all the smaller rodeos for practice and went to Cheyenne for the first events of the World Series. The Frontier Day rodeo was a five day affair held in July. In 1925 steer roping was the outstanding event of the show and at no place in the world was there so many "crack" ropers. Substantial money prizes were offered for the best roping during the five days of the rodeo. This was a time event with the championship being determined by the best time made on the steers. Each cowboy furnished his own horses for the roping and drew lots for the outlaws in the bucking contest. In roping, the steers were given a start of 30 feet. The contestants had to catch the animals by the horns or around the neck and throw and hog-tie him with three feet crossed.

There is no event of the rodeo that requires more strength or daring than the bulldogging contest. The steers are given a start of 30 feet on the wrestlers. The contestant is assisted by another mounted man, called the hazer, who helps to keep the steer running on a straight course but who cannot assist the bulldoger in any other way. Riding at full speed, the cowboy comes along the side of the fleeing steer and throws himself from his horse onto the horns of the animal. The wrestler must bring him to a dead stop and throw him flat on his side, holding him until the judges signal for the release. The contestant uses his hands only in the "twistdown" and cannot trip or "houlihan" his steer. This is also a time event determined by the average time on three steers.

Other events of the Cheyenne rodeo, but not counting toward the all-round cowboy championship, are the relay race, wild horse race, bareback riding, cow pony race, etc.

The 1925 rodeo at Cheyenne was held in a municipally owned park equipped with stands of steel and concrete seating 20,000 persons. Mayor Archie Allison of Cheyenne and Mayor Benjamin F. Stapleton of Denver clasped hands before the big crowd in the grandstand, signifying the goodwill between the two Western cities. Mable Strickland, astride one of her beautiful horses and carrying the American flag, led the grand procession that formally let down the bars of the rodeo. Governor Nellie T. Ross was second in the monster parade of cowboys and cowgirls on the park track.

Twenty-five events were held each day with about 200 of the best ranch folks in America participating. Bob Crosby won prizes in both steer roping and bulldogging. He took first place, the silver cup, and 100 points in the steer wrestling and went on to Pendleton for the last half of the contest for world championship cowboy. At the Pendleton Round-up he was third in both steer roping and in bulldogging. This gave him more than any man in the two contests, and he was proclaimed World's Champion All-round Cowboy.

As world champion cowboy and holder of the Roosevelt Trophy, Bob's services were in great demand at all the rodeos. Having the greatest cowboy in the world at the rodeo was like having Babe Ruth at a ball game or Jack Dempsey at a prize fight.

In 1926 Bob went to the Sesquicentennial Exposition at Philadelphia and carried off a large part of the prize money there. Among those who took part in the Sesquicentennial rodeo were Mable Strickland, Hugh Strickland, Chester Byers, Buck Stuart, Mike Hastings, Bryan Roach, Thad Lucas, and about 30 other cowboys and cowgirls.

From Philadelphia, Crosby went to Cedar Rapids, Iowa, for the Frontier Day celebration. A special train took the contestants from the Quaker City to Cedar Rapids. Other cowboy and cowgirls came on fresh from the big contest at Cheyenne, and the cowboy from the Staked Plains found himself in competition with a lot of new champions as well as the old crowd. In the Cheyenne group, and participating only in the women's events, was a 17 year old girl, Grace

Runyon, who had won the cowgirls' bucking contest. It was a great sight to see her curls fly as her outlaw, "Rawlins Kid," hit the ground stiff legged at Cedar Rapids.

Charlie Irwin managed the rodeo. Charlie Frazer's 21 piece band, a military band from Ft. Des Moines, and an Indian band from South Dakota furnished the music. The bucking horses came from Ismay, Montana; and there were plenty of famous outlaws in the string. The horses and cattle were rested and carefully fed so as to put them in first class condition for the rodeo.

Among the picturesque characters was "Hard Luck" Ike, who had lost a leg riding broncs. He bought him a wooden one and came on to Cedar Rapids to try anything offered. He was billed to ride a buffalo bull. Ike kept his seat just three jumps before taking flight to *tierra firma.*

"Can Crosby maintain his record as world's champion cowboy?" was the question asked by both spectators and cowboys at Cedar Rapids. Ed Bowman, roping wizard from Safford, Arizona, became Crosby's rival for roping honors. Slim Claskey crowded him closely for first place in bulldogging, the feat the cowboy had scored highest in during the World Series contests.

The Frontier Day celebration entered its final stage with Crosby in the lead in bulldogging with a low time record of 90.1 seconds. Claskey's time was 122.7 seconds, close enough for him to still win if Bob drew an especially tough critter or made any kind of fumble. The winner was to get $60 per day for day money and 60 per cent of a $700 prize.

Crosby had dropped to second in the roping but still had a chance to come out first. Bob's roping time for the week was 110.7 seconds as opposed to Bowman's 88.2.

There was a record breaking attendance for the finishing day. Crosby carried off first money in bulldogging. Claskey could not overcome the lead that Bob gained when he down-ed a big steer right in front of the grandstand in 16.2 second. Bowman cleaned up on the world's champion in calf roping, however, when he tied the world's record and wrapped up his calf in 16 seconds flat.

Failure to go to Cheyenne caused Bob Crosby to forfeit the 1926 championship to Norman Cowan of California. Four men had now won the Annual Roosevelt Trophy, and no cowboy had been able to take it the second time. With a new world champion in the field, Bob's popularity began to decline; and he made preparations to reestablish his supremacy.

The 1927 championship was the hardest contest of Bob Crosby's entire career. That year the cowboy from the Staked Plains had to beat three world champions and three newcomers of the highest order. They were Yakima Canutt of Washington, great bronc rider and original winner of the Roosevelt Trophy; Paddy Ryan, genial Irish peeler from Miles City, Montana, and 1924 world champion cowboy; Norman Cowan, steer twister and 1926 world champion cowboy.

The others were Hugh Strickland, who had a few championships in bygone years and who come to Pendleton from Cheyenne as second highest man. He had won his points on steer roping and bronc riding. Crosby had earned his as a steer roper and steer bulldogger. Dick Shelton of Ft. Worth, a rank stranger at Cheyenne, had finished third with 100 points toward the highest honors of all-round cowboy. Norman Cowan, world champion title holder, was fourth at Cheyenne with 90 points. Buck Lucas of Ft. Worth was also there with 80 points toward the Roosevelt Trophy.

Canutt and Ryan, both former world champion all-round cowboys, were farther down on the list of those who qualified at Cheyenne. They had copped their share of the firsts in previous years, however, and two firsts or a first and a second at Pendleton might again give either the world championship. Bob Crosby had finished first at Cheyenne, but this was the toughest mass of competition he ever faced.

When it was all over at Pendleton, Crosby was again World Champion All-round Cowboy. He boosted his score to the high mark by taking first place in the steer roping events. Ed Bowman of Safford, Arizona was announced world champion calf roper; Dick Shelton of Ft. Worth won the bulldogging contest; and Jesse Lawrence was proclaimed bucking horse champion. Josephine Wick of Colorado Springs, Colo., won the crown as world champion cowgirl. The *vaquero* from the Staked Plains had done what no other cowboy had ever done—become the world champion cowboy for the second time. Along with the Roosevelt trophy, he received a silver mounted saddle, inlaid with gold and carried away cash prizes ranging up to $1,400 he received for first in steer roping.

During the next season, Bob Crosby contested in 23 rodeos. He opened at Phoenix, Ariz., and played the following towns in order—Ft. Worth, Texas; Wickenberg, Ariz.; Brawley, Calif.; Sylvan Beach, Texas; Los Angeles, Calif.; Columbus, Ohio; Buffalo, N. Y.; Toronto, Ont.; Calgary, Alberta; Cheyenne, Wyoming; Kingman, Kans.; Kiowa, Okla.; Chicago, Ill.; Sumas, Wash.; Ellenburg, Wash.; Pendleton, Ore.; Wiser, Idaho; Montreal, Quebec; Detroit, Mich.; New York City; and Floydada, Texas. His earnings for the season were $14,915 in the form of prizes. Bob said that his horse, "Nickel Grabber", was entitled to half the honors.

During the next season, Bob and "Nickel Grabber" went to Salt Lake City and grabbed some more nickels. They scooped up $1,500 and three championships in this big city in the heart of the West. Crosby was 28 when he took first place in steer roping, calf roping, and bulldogging in the Mormon city.

Roy Kivet, a favorite with the cowboys and cowgirls, was killed the first day of the rodeo when his horse fell on him while he was roping a steer. This dampened the ardor of many of the contestants. The more superstitious declared there would be three serious accidents, and two or three flatly refused to enter certain events. One bronc peeler who had never been known to turn down a horse said: "No, sir! I am not going to ride that horse. One of us has got to follow Roy, and it's not goin' to be me."

Bob went on but got a bad eye when a big steer objected to having his neck twisted and hooked his horn in the cowboy's left orb. No permanent injury resulted, however.

Bob Crosby rode in 12 events during the four days of Salt Lake rodeo and carried home a white Tom Mix hat, a pair of cowboy boots, an all wool riding vest, and other prizes in addition to $1,500 in cash. His average time for bulldogging was 21 seconds; calf roping, 25 seconds; and steer roping, 26 seconds. Mrs. Crosby usually accompanied her husband, and she and Roberta were with him at Salt Lake.

The Crosbys had built an attractive home in Abilene, Texas. After a few weeks at home and visits to San Angelo, Bob loaded "Bullet", another of his fine horses, into a trailer, hitched the trailer on behind a new Buick and headed for the Stampede at Calgary, Alberta, Canada. He came back a little later with his share of the bacon and classing the Calgary Stampede with the best rodeos in the United States.

The variation in the names of the celebrations is noticeable. At Cheyenne, it is a "rodeo". At Pendleton, it is a "round-up"; at Calgary, a "stampede". In Australia, it is a "muster."

The Spanish Southwest was the first real cattle country in America, and Southwestern ranchers prefer the Spanish word "rodeo". It is the noun for the verb *rodear,* meaning to surround or enclose.

The rodeos of Spain are closely related to the bull ring. A horseman, armed with a steel pointed lance, enters the ring alone with an infurated bull and tries to kill the animal without getting hurt. He rides round and round, or "roderlo". The horses are often gored, and sometimes the matadors lose their lives.

The racing receives a little more emphasis at Calgary. Perhaps it is the disorderly chuck wagon and cow pony races, with the attendant noise, that reminds the Canadians of a stampede.

When the 1928 rodeo season rolled around, there was danger of a new contestant taking Bob's title as world champion cowboy. He decided to again enter the Cheyenne and Pendleton contests, and put a stop to this danger for all time by winning permanent possession of the Roosevelt Trophy.

Canutt, Ryan, and Cowan, former world champion cowboys, had already been defeated twice by Crosby and were not likely to be dangerous opposition; but Ed Bowman, world champion calf roper, and Dick Shelton, champion bulldogger, were the highest types of competition.

Bob Crosby was 31 years old and weighed 190 pounds when he went back to Cheyenne and Pendleton to win permanent possession of the Roosevelt Trophy, a prize that no other cowboy had ever won the second time. His height was 5 feet 10 inches.

The 1928 purses at Pendleton were as follows: steer roping, $1,400; bucking contest for championship of the world, $900; calf roping, $750; steer bulldogging, $750; cowboys' pony race, $200; stage coach race, $600; Indian pony race, $200; pony express race, $500; cowgirls' pony race, $200; Indian pony relay race, $300; bucking horse contest of the Northwest, $500; cowgirls' relay race, $100.

As usual, only points in bucking, steer roping, and bull-dogging counted toward the world championship as all-round cowboy. From the beginning, the contest was a struggle between Crosby from New Mexico, Bowman from Arizona, and Shelton from Texas. Bowman had beaten Crosby on calves, but Bob did not think he could do it on steers. Shelton and Crosby were closely matched on bull-dogging, the result probably depended on the animals they drew. Norman Cowan and Truck Greenough battled for the bucking championship and a chance at the all-round cowboy crown.

Thirty-two thousand rodeo fans witnessed the finish of the Pendleton rodeo. It wound up in a whirlwind of flying hoofs, bucking horses, and wide-eyed steers. There were spilled jockeys, thrown bronc peelers, overturned chuck wagons, etc., that kept the stretcher bearer busy. The hardiest riders of the range were out for the championships and were ready to sacrifice skin and bones to get them.

It was a corking good show, full of action. Two cowboys in the pony races fought with their quirts as they raced. Another who was booed by the grandstand retaliated by thumbing his nose at the spectators. Donna Cowan's horse threw her; and two Indians bit the dust, one receiving serious injuries. An Indian maid defeated all the white-faced girls in a foot race. Bronc peelers who kept their seats earned their rides, and more than one soared spread-eagle through the air. Those who craved action got it, from the time the first Brahma bull romped out from under his rider until the grand finale that decided the bronc riding campionship of the world.

Not until the last minute of the Round-up was it determined that Bob Crosby had again won the title of world's champion all-round cowboy. He cinched the championship by roping and tying three big steers in 1 minute and 6 4-5 seconds. The cowboy of the Staked Plains had tied up three 4-year-old steers as quickly as a Woolworth girl bags a baby's rattler. He also won the world's championship as a calf roper by tying his three calves in 62 2-5 seconds. He bulldogged a steer in 18 seconds.

Dick Shelton was second high in the all-round cowboy championship. Everett Bowman was third.

Shelton became the world's champion bulldogger. His best time was 18 4-5 seconds. Tuck Greenough was winner of the cowboy's bucking contest.

Mable Strickland won the cowgirl's relay race. The distance was 1 and 1-2 miles. Three horses were used, and she had to dismount and change ponies every half mile.

The brass bands ceased to play. The rumble of the stage coaches died away, and the dust began to settle over the arena. The 19th annual roundup was over; and Bob Crosby, rider of the Staked Plains, was world champion cowboy for all time. No other cowboy had ever won the Roosevelt trophy twice, to say nothing of winning it a third time. It was now Bob's for keeps.

Most of the visitors left Pendleton that evening or early the next morning. Bob Crosby and his wife and daughter stayed over to attend church. Bob is a member of the Christian Church, and not once during the five years he had contested at Pendleton had he missed attending church there.

By request of the Rev. G. L. Drill, Bob took the beautiful Roosevelt Trophy to church with him. The minister chose as the subject of his sermon, "The Secret of a Glad Heart", holding the clean sportsmanship and happy smile of the cowboy up as an example of the lesson he was delivering. In the course of his talk he declared that Bob Crosby had proven that any man can mingle in worldly affairs even when his surroundings are of the most unrestrained in character and still retain his high ideals and respect for sacred things. He further stated:

"This man is the World Champion All-round Cowboy, the winner of the beautiful trophy you see here. Despite the environment which his vocation forces upon him, he does not use strong drink or tobacco in any form. He does not use coffee because he thinks that it will have an unsteadying effect on his nerves. This young man, he is only 31 years old, tells me that no person can use stimulants and continue to win constantly as a round-up performer.

"He is always smiling happily. His life is the secret of his glad heart. Is it not the glad heart of a Christian cowboy that has enabled him to come back twice since his initial victory and finally win the coveted trophy which he now owns permanently and is carrying back with him to his ranch in New Mexico?"

He might have added that Bob's dissipation consists chiefly of gum chewing. Sometimes when catapulted from the hurricane deck of a broncho, as happens occasionally to the best of riders, he would calmly arise from the dust with his jaws working.

Simplicity was the style for his dress. Blue denim trousers, work shirt, and black hat, battered by the gales of the Staked Plains, formed his makeup when he stood before the grandstand to receive the 1927 trophy from George Baer. It was typical of his dress on the home range and in the arena.

Bob Crosby seldom wore chaps. Even the red bandana was absent from his neck. When not riding the range or contesting at rodeos, he usually wore a dark suit, soft hat, and white shirt. He stayed at first class hotels and drove medium priced automobiles. He was a careful driver. In fact, he was a practical cattleman.

The cowboy of the Staked Plains came out of the Pendleton Round-up with the title of world champion steer roper and world champion calf roper as well as the all-round cowboy trophy. No one could ever take the Roosevelt trophy from him, but many persons tried to beat him in various events. One of the hardest contests Crosby ever had was a calf roping competition with Jake McClure of Lovington, N. M., another cowboy of the Staked Plains. Jake McClure was born at Amarillo, Texas, November 26, 1902. He worked for the Matadors, the Slaughter Cattle Co., and other first class outfits before starting a spread of his own in Lea County, New Mexico. He entered his first rodeo at Roswell, N. M., in 1925. He wrapped up his dogie in 16.5 seconds at the Calgary Stampeed, and soon won the world's championship at Pendleton. He had a lot of fast ties to his credit, and many believed he could beat Crosby. Prosser Martin, cowboy outfitter of Del Rio, Texas, worked up a match between the world champion all-round cowboy and the world chamuion calf roper with a $2,500 prize at stake.

McClure had taken every big calf roping event of the year when he went to the town on the Rio Grande to compete with Crosby. At the Chicago championship rodeo he had lowered the world's calf roping record by tying his critter in 13 seconds flat. The match at Del Rio called for the roping of 50 calves each, enough to eliminate most of the hazards of luck. In order that there should be no difference in the calves, both men roped the same animals. Each man roped 25 the first day and then took his opponent's 25 for the second.

This was the most important roping match held since Bert Weir of Monument, N. M., also of the Llano Estacado, beat Rafael Fraustro, champion steer roper of Mexico, in a contest at Juarez.

Much of the results of any roping depends on the horse; and Crosby and McClure, of course, rode the best horses in their strings. Crosby used "Scar Face," a horse he had raised from a dogie colt. He weighed 1,075 when in good condition. McClure's mount, "Legs", was a little heavier.

There is considerable difference between a good calf roping mount and a steer roping horse. Roping procedure varies a little in different parts of the country; but as a general rule in steer roping, the rope is thrown over the animal's rear axle after he has been roped by the horns or around the neck and the horse is run by him. Having caught the steer by the head and the rope going over behind him, all four feet can be jerked from under the critter. The horse, with his tail toward the steer, keeps pulling when the animal tries to get up. In calf roping, the instant the calf is caught, the horse is stopped; and the roper jumps off and throws the animal himself. The horse keeps the rope tight by backing up. Few horses are equally good on both steers and calves.

Texas, and some other states, have abolished steer roping on the ground that it is cruel. Many cattlemen have supported the move because their stock suffered from ropers practicing on them. It does not seem to hurt a calf much to rope and flank him down, but often the only way a big steer can be kept down long enough to tie him is to throw him so hard that he is temporarily knocked out.

At the end of the first day of roping at Del Rio, Crosby had a lead of 52 3-5 seconds. Think of two men roping 25 calves with less than a minute's difference in their time! Bob Crosby caught his 25 calves without missing a throw with the rope. McClure missed three times. Crosby also made the best single roping of the day by tying a calf in 18 seconds flat.

Although Del Rio is on the Rio Grande, about half way between El Paso and the Gulf, 2 inches of snow fell the first day of the contest and slowed down the performance. Crosby, because of his weight, seemed to have the advantage in handling the calves. Bob's slowest record was 35 1-5 seconds, while McClure consumed 52 2-5 seconds in roping and tying a calf after he had missed one loop. Still, 52 seconds is not a hopeless lead when there are 25 calves yet to be tied up. McClure apparently had drawn the larger and faster calves the first day, and his supporters predicted that he would clean up on the champion all-round cowboy the second day when the calves would be reversed. McClure's average was a little over 25 seconds per calf, while Crosby's was about 23 seconds.

Before the match was over, Allen Holder of Rankin, Texas, challenged the winner for a contest to be held 15 days later at Abilene for a $1,500 purse.

On the second day, Crosby took the 25 calves that McClure had roped; and McClure took Crosby's calves. McClure opened up Monday by tying a calf in 17 seconds, the fastest time made during the two days of roping. His slowest time was 31 3-5 seconds; and spectators began to say, "See! Crosby had the easy calves!"

Crosby missed a loop on his 19th calf and had a time record of 42 2-5 seconds to mar his second day's performance. Try as hard as he could, he was unable to duplicate McClure's time of 17 seconds. Crosby and "Scar Face" fought desperately to hold their lead. Bob's lead slowly disappeared. "Scar Face" outdid "Legs" in the heavy mud, but his master was penalized 30 seconds for infractions of the rules. This hurt badly until McClure, also, drew a penalty of 20 seconds and evened the score up again somewhat.

As they neared the end of the contest, McClure was not 5 seconds behind. Crosby roped his last calf, and McClure was where another 17 second record would make him winner. Crosby held his breath while McClure raced after the last calf with all the skill of a great roper. When the last calf was tied, the world's champion cowboy had beaten the world's champion calf roper by the narrow margin of 2.5 seconds!

Crosby met Allen Holder at Abilene a few weeks later and beat him 45.3 seconds on 19 calves, without counting the 20th, which was a fumble for Holder.

Crosby went home with the prize money, but when asked who was the best calf roper the Staked Plains ever had, he replied that it was his neighbor, Jake McClure.

Bob thought old "Midnight", discovered by Pete Welch of Calgary, Alberta, was the worst piece of horse flesh that ever shook a saddle. When "Midnight" came down to the Cheyenne rodeo in 1932, several great bronc peelers were hoping to ride to the world's championship on his back. The reputation of this fighting outlaw was already so well established that it was generally conceded that whoever drew him would probably become the new world's champion if he could keep his seat. When the drawing was over, the job had fallen to Bob Askins, a man who had already won the world's champion as a bronc peeler in previous contests. Some said the horse was lame and would be easy for Askins. Others thought the mud would slow "Midnight" down, and winning the world's championship might be easy. Askins believed the world's only unrideable horse would soon be ridden. When news spread that the man who had already won the world's championship had drawn "Midnight", the excitement became intense and the betting ran high. At last all was in readiness for the biggest event of the Cheyenne rodeo. The man at chute number 3 gave a mighty tug that opened the gate and fled for safety. Inside was "Midnight", the fightin'est *cayuse* that ever pawed the sod at old Cheyenne. On his back was Bob Askins, as good a bronc buster as ever dug spurs into horse flesh.

For a few seconds old "Midnight" stood stock still with his head up. Perhaps he was waiting for the photographers to get a good picture of Napoleon before Waterloo. Askins gave him the rowels. "Midnight's" head went down as he cleared the chute with a mighty leap. Soon Askin's arms were flying as though he were flailing wheat. His head jerked in all directions. The stop watch ticked an eternally long 2 seconds, and the bronc peeler was still on board. At the end of 2.8 seconds, "Midnight" was weaving as though twisted by a cyclone; and Askins was still being flailed by the gale. At 3.8 the bronc buster toppled but seemed to regain his balance. Midnight seemed to think the show had lasted long enough. With a final contortion, and a resounding whack on the broad seat of Askins' pants with the cantle board, "Five Minutes to Midnight" made a spread-eagle out of the world champion bronc peeler.

"Was anybody killed when the lightning struck?" the ex-champion asked. He had landed feet first. His question was drowned by the mighty cheer that Midnight received. The horse, his proud head up, galloped triumphantly out of the arena, his fighting spirit still unconquered.

Again, in 1936, "Midnight" pawed at the bars of the Cheyenne corrals. Nick Knight of Cody, Wyoming, a new knight of the bucking arena, drew him. Wyoming rooters thought it was the dark hour before the dawn when their Knight took his seat on "Midnight." Again "Midnight" delayed his action while he concocted some diabolic amusement for the benefit of the grandstand. When he finally jumped, it was good night for Mr. Knight. The outlaw broke the altitude record at the first leap. At the next jump he kicked the horns off the moon. As "Midnight" stood on his head, the Knight did a "shoot the chute", and that was the end of the story of the Knight who went riding at midnight!

Crosby made it a rule to sell any horse he had when the animal became worth $500. Consequently, he was always training new mounts. He considered "Nickel Grabber" the best steer roping horse in his string. It was "Nickel" who won the steer roping championship of the world at Pendleton in 1927. "Scar Face" was the best of his calf roping animals. It was "Scar Face" who helped him to rope and tie more calves than Jake McClure, the world's champion calf roper, in the contest at Del Rio.

Probably the best saddle ever made to Bob Crosby's specifications was the roping model made by Prosser Martin of Del Rio, Texas. There is a difference between roping saddles and bucking saddles. The roping saddle has a low cantle that facilitates dismounting. The bucking saddles are just the reverse. They have high cantles and more or less swell forks to make unseating as difficult as possible.

The Crosby saddle made by Martin had a 12 inch fork, 14½ inch seat, 2 inch Cheyenne cantle, and a 2¼ inch horn. It weighed 37 pounds complete and ready to ride. It was finished in hand tooled black and tan leather. The corners were ornamented with tooled pictures of Crosby in action, copied from photographs. The jockey on the left bore a Masonic square and compass. The other jockey carried the scimitar and crescent of the Shrine. The cowboy was a member of both orders. His name, with the legend, "World's Champion Cowboy", was lettered on the stirrup leathers.

Winning prizes at the smaller rodeos was a snap for Bob Crosby. After being laid up with rheumatism for several months, he went up to Sun City, Kansas, for a workout. A few days later he wired his wife: "Won everything except the grandstand". He had taken first in all the main events.

On another occasion he and "Brezy" Cox of Solomonville, Arizona, went to a rodeo in Nebraska disguised as drugstore cowboys. They arrived a little late, but since no one objected to the entrance of the boys wearing low quarter shoes, the manager accepted their entrance fees and let them participate. When the time came to settle up, Crosby and Cox drew 80 per cent of the prize money.

With the Roosevelt Trophy, the highest award of the rodeo world, his for keeps, and with his earnings increasing, Bob Crosby went to Prescott, Arizona, for the annual Frontier Day Rodeo in 1930. This was in the heart of the Arizona cattle country and drew a heavy attendance from Phoenix as well as locally. While contesting there, he drew an exceptionally heavy brute in the bulldogging. The steer was traveling like an express train when the cowboy threw himself from the saddle onto the animal's horns. As Crosby dug his heels into the ground to bring the beast to a stop, the weight of the animal crumpled the cowboy's leg. In spite of the pain, Crosby threw the steer. When the judges had approved the twistdown, Bob got up and hobbled over to the sidelines and sat down. Several cowboys passed without realizing the world champion had been seriously injured. At last a Boy Scout called an ambulance, and Bob Crosby was taken to a hospital. Infection set in. Physicians said his leg would have to be amputated. Crosby thought any kind of leg would beat a wooden one. Then came a long fight to retain the injured limb. After several operations, he went to Winslow, Arizona with his leg in steel braces. He would rope his calf, dismount, hop along the rope until he could reach the animal and throw and tie it. In spite of the injury, he made $500 at the Winslow rodeo.

Bob never wholly recovered from this injury. In spite of this handicap, he continued to take part in many of the major rodeo events of the nation during the next 16 years. During that time he met most of the best steer and calf ropers of the world in privately sponsored matches. He did not win all of them, but he won such a large majority of the matches that he became wealthy. In 1937 he bought the E. L. McBryde ranch 15 miles south of Elida, New Mexico.

About the same time he built a lovely home on the north banks of North Spring River at Roswell, a town long famous as headquarters for wealthy cattlemen. This beautiful structure in the northwest part of the city was California-Spanish in its architectual design and stood on an elevation that gave excellent view of the pretty stream with its fine homes and delightful drives.

In September, 1946, the author watched Bob Crosby beat Jack Hitson of Fort Sumner, New Mexico, for the major portion of a $1,000 purse in a steer roping contest at Tucumcari, N. Mex., sponsored by the Lions Club. A sandstorm was sweeping across the arena where the Quay County Sheriff's Posse holds it annual rodeo, and both men were slower than they ordinarily would have been. Hampered by the strong wind, both had to get in close before throwing their ropes. Bob's final counting was 414.8 to Hitson's 501.9 for roping and tying 12 steers each. It was a good show; but it was plain that age, more weight, the bad leg, and the sandstorm had slowed down the world's champion. Bob was not as spectacular as he was in younger days.

A few week later the world's champion all-round cowboy was beaten by Lewis Cooper in a 20 steer match at the Roosevelt Country Fair at Portales, New Mexico. Cooper, a Kenna, N. Mex., cattleman and neighbor to Crosby's old home ranch, beat the famous all-round cowboy with a margin of 53.9 seconds or less than a minute on roping and tying 20 steers.

Bob was scheduled for one more roping match for 1946. He announced that he would retire when that was over. He went down to Carlsbad determined to wind up his career with victory or bust a hame string. At the "Cavern City" he met for the second time Bert Weir of Monument, New Mexico, another Staked Plains cowboy with a nationwide reputation as a roper. Bob put everything he had into this final roping match. Bob had an old, battered black hat that he wore the season he first won the world's championship at Cheyenne and Pendelton. It had become his lucky charm, and he put it on for this final play in his roping career. Luck rode again with the old black hat, and Crosby checked out his 16 steers and two days of roping with a substantial margin over Weir.

Bob went back to his home at Roswell and was killed a few months later in a car wreck while on his way to the old home ranch near Kenna.

This unpretentious rider of the Staked Plains made quite a contrast with the movie heros and the wild cow pokes of the "bang, bang" magazines. Yes, stranger, he looked about as much like a movie hero as a range bronc looks like a polo horse. But there was no mistaking the fact that he was a real cowboy, and the best of them all. The judges at Cheyenne and Pendleton made quite certain of that in three annual roundups in which Crosby beat as talented a bunch of *hombres* as ever forked a *cayuse* or tied a cow critter.

The romance and colorful clothes of the cinema were not for Bob. He did not wear hairy chaps with pounds of brass embellishments. There was no silk bandana at this throat, nor were his shirts of the convential bright color. His hat wouldn't hold ten gallons, but it topped a pretty competent dome. People sometimes said he didn't look his part, but that he was the greatest all-round cowboy, few ever disputed.

As astonishing as were his habilaments, the record of his private life was quite as singular. He was a quiet mannered cattleman, happily married and possessed of fine children. He liked clean sport. He stayed home at night. His days were as calm and uneventual as yours. Yes, sir, he was "on the reservation" all the time; and you'd have to ride far, stranger, to find a better type of westerner.

—177—

Well, facts are stranger than fiction, and certainly in fiction stories, the cowboy is surprisingly unlike Bob Crosby. The fictional cowboy goes about his affairs just a jump ahead of the sheirff's posse, with pungency of powder smoke in his nostrils. Seems like he can't ride into Tombstone or Old Cheyenne to licker up or play a little faro, but that some renegade throws down on him, and he has to shoot his way out. The result is that the fictional cowboy is in the saddle most of the time racing with lead instead of after cattle. Of course, all who read fiction know that all will be well with the hero in the end and that he will never stretch hemp nor stop a .44 slug. It's a cinch he'll marry the pretty school m'am and save the Cross-L Ranch, even if he has to shoot his way to happiness.

We prefer to remember the world's greatest all-round cowboy as he really was, happy, even tempered, capable Bob Crosby.

The End

WORLD CHAMPION COWBOYS SINCE 1948

ALL-AROUND CHAMPIONS

1956 Jim Shoulders, Henryetta, Okla.

1955 Casey Tibbs, Ft. Pierre, South Dakota

1954 Buck Rutherford, Lenapah, Okla.

1953 Bill Linderman, Red Lodge, Montana

1952 Harry Tompkins, Dublin, Texas

1951 Casey Tibbs, Ft. Pierre, South Dakota

1950 Bill Linderman, Red Lodge, Montana

1949 Jim Shoulders, Tulsa, Okla.

1948 Gerald Roberts, Strong City, Kansas

BAREBACK RIDING

1956 Jim Shoulders, Henryetta, Okla.

1955 Eddy Akridge, Hesperia, Calif.

1954 Eddy Akridge, Gruver, Tex.

1953 Eddy Akridge, Gruver, Tex.

1952 Harry Tompkins, Dublin, Texas

1951 Casey Tibbs, Ft. Pierre, South Dakota

1950 Jim Shoulders, Tulsa, Okla.

1949 Jack Buschbom, Cassville, Wisconsin

1948 Sonny Tureman, Pueblo, Colorado

STEER WRESTLING

1956 Harley May, Deming, N.M.

1955 Benny Combs, Checotah, Okla.

1954 James Bynum, Waxahachie, Texas

1953 Ross Dollarhide, Lake View, Oregon

1952 Harley May, Deming, N.M.

1951 Dub Phillips, San Angelo, Texas

1950 Bill Linderman, Red Lodge, Montana

1949 Bill McGuire, Ft. Worth, Texas

1948 Homer Pettigrew, Grady, New Mexico

SADDLE BRONC RIDING

1956 Deb Copenhaver, Post Falls, Idaho

1955 Deb Copenhaver, Post Falls, Idaho

1954 Casey Tibbs, Ft. Pierre, South Dakota

1953 Casey Tibbs, Ft. Pierre, South Dakota

1952 Casey Tibbs, Ft. Pierre, South Dakota

1951 Casey Tibbs, Ft. Pierre, South Dakota

1950 Bill Linderman, Red Lodge, Montana

1949 Casey Tibbs, Ft. Pierre, South Dakota

1948 Gene Pruitt, Yakima, Wash.

BULL RIDING	CALF ROPING
1956 Jim Shoulders, Henryetta, Okla.	1956 Ray Wharton, Bandera, Texas
1955 Jim Shoulders, Henryetta, Okla.	1955 Dean Oliver, Nampa, Idaho
1954 Jim Shoulders, Tulsa, Okla.	1954 Don McLaughlin, Smithfield, Texas
1953 Todd Whatley, Hugo, Okla.	1953 Don McLaughlin, Smithfield, Texas
1952 Harry Tompkins, Dublin, Texas	1952 Don McLaughlin, Ft. Worth, Texas
1951 Jim Shoulders, Tulsa, Okla.	1951 Don McLaughlin, Ft. Worth, Texas
1950 Harry Tompkins, Dublin, Texas	1950 Toots Mansfield, Big Spring, Texas
1949 Harry Tompkins, Ardmore, Okla.	1949 Troy Fort, Lovington, N. M.
1948 Harry Tompkins, Ardmore, Okla.	1948 Toots Mansfield, Bandera, Texas